Standing Again

Healing, Health, and
Our Inner Light

KB212404

Standing Again

Healing, Health, and Our Inner Light

Dharma Talks by Seon Master Daehaeng
English translation and editing by
Hanmaum International Culture Institute
Cover design by Su Yeon Park
Published by Hanmaum Publications

First edition, first printing: January 2019

within Korea
tel: (031)470-3175 / fax: (031)470-3209
Outside Korea
tel: (82-31)470-3175 / fax: (82-31)470-3209
E-mail: onemind@hanmaum.org

ISBN 978-89-91857-54-4 (03220)

국립중앙도서관 출판예정도서목록(CIP)

Standing Again : Healing, health, and our inner light /
Dharma talks by Seon Master Daehaeng ; English translati
on and editing by Hanmaum International Culture Institut
e. -- [Anyang] : Hanmaum publications, 2019
    p. ;   cm

Translated from Korean
ISBN   978-89-91857-54-4 03220 : US$12.95

225.2-KDC6
294.34-DDC23   CIP2018040255

A CIP catalogue record of the National Library of Korea for this
book is available at the homepage of CIP(http://seoji.nl.go.kr)
and Korean Library Information System Network(http://www.
nl.go.kr/kolisnet). (CIP2018040255)

Standing Again

Healing, Health, and Our Inner Light

Seon Master Daehaeng

foreword by Menas Kafatos

Contents

The One that is Truly Doing

Who is the one that enables us to see?

Who is the one that enables us to hear?

Who is the one that enables us to speak?

Who is the one that enables us to live?

Observe, observe, and observe again.

You, observing,

are true self.

People think that we see because we have eyes,

but is this true?

People think that we hear because we have ears,

but is this true?

People think that we speak because we have a mouth,

but is this true?

People think that we live because we have a body,

but is this true?

Observe, observe, and observe again.

You, observing,

are true self.

—Daehaeng Kun Sunim

Foreword

What is incredible about this collection of Dharma talks by Seon Master Daehaeng is how down to earth her talks are, yet they contain such sublime teachings for all humanity.

She draws our attention to what seemingly makes no sense — the suffering of human life and the unpredictability of what may happen at any time to our health and well-being. She points us to basic, related truths that we seem to be missing: The countless beings that make up our bodies, the role of karma, and its nature, and the relevance of what is called "emptiness."

She provides a very practical way to address these, and the prescription is the same: Rely on your fundamental mind which works with the foundation of the entire universe. In other words, bring in the vast power of the universe which is yours. She gives us a new perspective to the whole issue of healing, releasing the past, and not being afraid of the future. Healing is just a moment away, if what I may call grace, the connection to our fundamental nature, is allowed to do its work.

As a scientist, I find her direct approach to be truly scientific in the full sense of the word. It is based in experience, in observing how things truly are. Even though human life seems so fragile — it can end so quickly — yet we carry with us eons of evolution, the eternity of existence. Why not try to have this attitude, even though we know that one day it will all end? We are here on the earthly plane to go higher or lower, the choice is ours. Heaven and hell are right here, it is our choice to go higher if we have the right attitude. This is the true science of right living, of healthy living and Seon Master Daehaeng shows us the vision. Going beyond what we think should be, the vision of entrusting our true nature, no matter what, is a true hope for right living.

In the questions and answers that follow her talk, she points out that if science just relies on physical aspects, then karmic links and entanglements cannot be resolved. As a scientist, I hear what she says: We are way beyond a mere physical existence. This is the meaning of what Deepak Chopra and I wrote in our book *You Are the Universe*. Fear and names of diseases do a lot of harm until we realize our unity with everything else, until we realize that "me" and "others" are just aspects of our fundamental nature. As she points out, the five subtle powers in themselves don't take us very far. Our disparate parts coming together, realizing that diseases may have different origins and reasons of manifestation, we can move beyond the ordinary appearances to the realm of true healing, to the inner "captain," our Buddha nature.

These dharma talks open doors for science to flourish and human beings to advance. They provide a scientific method for the future by a great Seon Master, combining science and spirituality to live a practical healthy life. The new book certainly opened doors for me to see things in a much clearer way. I am grateful for her continuous love for humanity, for her continuous presence in my life. Her presence is indeed beyond space and time, beyond past and future. It is the true foundation of the cosmos.

Menas Kafatos
Fletcher Jones Endowed Chair Professor of
Computational Physics, Chapman University

About Daehaeng Kun Sunim

Daehaeng *Kun Sunim*[1](1927 - 2012) was a rare teacher in Korea: a female *Seon(Zen)*[2] master, a nun whose students also included monks, and a teacher who helped revitalize Korean Buddhism by dramatically increasing the participation of young people and men.

She broke out of traditional models of spiritual practice to teach in such a way that allowed anyone to practice and awaken, making laypeople a particular focus of her efforts. At the same time, she was a major force for the advancement of *Bhikkunis*,[3] heavily supporting traditional nuns' colleges as well as the modern Bhikkuni Council of Korea.

---

1. Sunim / Kun Sunim: Sunim is the respectful title of address for a Buddhist monk or nun in Korea, and Kun Sunim is the title given to outstanding nuns or monks.

2. Seon(禪)(Chan, Zen): Seon describes the unshakeable state where one has firm faith in their inherent foundation, their Buddha-nature, and so returns everything they encounter back to this fundamental mind. It also means letting go of "I," "me," and "mine" throughout one's daily life.

Born in Seoul, Korea, she awakened when she was around eight years old and spent the years that followed learning to put her understanding into practice. For years, she wandered the mountains of Korea, wearing ragged clothes and eating only what was at hand. Later, she explained that she hadn't been pursuing some type of asceticism; rather, she was just completely absorbed in entrusting everything to her fundamental *Buddha*[4] essence and observing how that affected her life.

Those years profoundly shaped Kun Sunim's later teaching style; she intimately knew the great potential, energy, and wisdom inherent within each of us, and recognized that most of the people she encountered suffered because they didn't realize

---

3. Bhikkunis: Female sunims who are fully ordained are called *Bhikkuni*(比丘尼) sunims, while male sunims who are fully ordained are called *Bhikku*(比丘) sunims. This can also be a polite way of indicating male or female sunims.

4. Buddha: In this text, "Buddha" is capitalized out of respect, because it represents the essence and function of the enlightened mind. "The Buddha" always refers to Sakyamuni Buddha.

this about themselves. Seeing clearly the great light in every individual, she taught people to rely upon this inherent foundation, and refused to teach anything that distracted from this most important truth.

Without any particular intention to do so, Daehaeng Kun Sunim demonstrated on a daily basis the freedom and ability that arise when we truly connect with this fundamental essence inherent within us.

The sense of acceptance and connection people felt from being around her, as well as the abilities she manifested, weren't things she was trying to show off. In fact, she usually tried to hide them because people would tend to cling to these, without realizing that chasing after them cannot lead to either freedom or awakening.

Nonetheless, in her very life, in everything she did, she was an example of the true freedom and wisdom that arise from this very basic, fundamental essence that we all have – that we are. She showed that because we are all interconnected, we can deeply understand what's going on with others, and that the intentions we give rise to can manifest and function in the world.

All of these are in a sense side effects, things that arise naturally when we are truly one with everyone and everything around us. They happen because we are able to flow in harmony with our world, with no dualistic views or attachments to get in the way. At this point, other beings are not cut off from us; they are another aspect of ourselves. Who, feeling this to their very bones, could turn their back on others?

It was this deep compassion that made her a legend in Korea long before she formally started teaching. She was known for having the spiritual power to help people in all circumstances and with every kind of problem. She compared compassion to freeing a fish from a drying puddle, putting a homeless family into a home, or providing the school fees that would allow a student to finish high school. And when she did things like this, and more, few knew that she was behind it.

Her compassion was also unconditional. She would offer what help she could to individuals and organizations, whether they be Christian or Buddhist, a private organization or governmental. She would help nun's temples that had no relationship with her temple, Christian organizations that looked after children living on their own, city-run projects to help care for the elderly, and much, much more. Yet, even when she provided material support, always there was the deep, unseen aid she offered through this connection we all share.

However, she saw that ultimately, for people to live freely and go forward in the world as a blessing to all around them, they needed to know about this bright essence that is within each of us. To help people discover this for themselves, she founded the first *Hanmaum*[5] Seon Center in 1972. For the next

---

5. Hanmaum [han-ma-um]: Han means one, great, and combined, while maum means mind, as well as heart, and together they mean everything combined and connected as one.

What is called Hanmaum is intangible, unseen, and transcends time and space. It has no beginning or end, and is sometimes called our fundamental mind. It also means the mind of all beings and everything in the universe connected and working together as one. In English, we usually translate this as one mind.

forty years she gave wisdom to those who needed wisdom, food and money to those who were poor and hungry, and compassion to those who were hurting.

Daehaeng Kun Sunim founded ten overseas branches of Hanmaum Seon Center, and her teachings have been translated into twelve different languages to date: English, German, Russian, Chinese, French, Spanish, Indonesian, Italian, Japanese, Vietnamese, Estonian, and Czech, in addition to the original Korean. For more information about these or the overseas centers, please see the back of this book.

Dharma Talk 1

The Doctor is In

December 20, 1992

This talk was first published in English
as Volume 15 in the ongoing series,
Practice in Daily Life.

It's always nice to be here together with you, and today seems particularly wonderful because so many people have come here from the branch temples. [Putting her hands together and bowing.] I see that we even have the choir from Daegu here as well!

You all know the Korean proverb, "Stick together and live. Scatter and die," right? Well, microbes as well as human beings are functioning like this. They all come into existence because earth, water, fire, and air gather together like this. In order for that to happen, there first has to be an affinity between both parents, as well as ourselves. Once that connects, all of our *karmic consciousnesses*,[6] both good and bad,

---

6. Karmic consciousness: Our thoughts, feelings, and behaviors are recorded as the consciousnesses of the lives that make up our body. These are sometimes called karmic consciousnesses, although they don't have independent awareness or volition. Sometime afterwards, these consciousnesses will come back out.

Thus, we may feel happy, sad, angry, etc., without an obvious reason, or they may cause other problems to occur. The way to dissolve these consciousnesses is not to react to them when they arise, but instead to entrust them to our foundation. However, even these consciousnesses are just temporary combinations, so we shouldn't cling to the concept of them.

gather together and then form a body, with which we are born into this world.

All of this is possible because of the gathering and scattering of the four elements. We could not have been born as human beings, nor could we communicate as we do, nor could we fulfill our role as the highest animal without the gathering and scattering of the four elements. Likewise, they form the basis of much of science and scientific research.

Our physical aspect is all based on the four elements, but what organizes and directs all this is our *fundamental mind*,[7] our Buddha-nature. Thus any kind of research or exploration has to include this fundamental mind; it has to be carried out at

---

7. Fundamental mind: This refers to our inherent essence, that which we fundamentally are. "Mind," in Mahayana Buddhism, almost never means the brain or intellect. Instead it refers to the essence through which we are connected to everything, everywhere. It is intangible, beyond space and time, and has no beginning or end. It is the source of everything, and everyone is endowed with it. "Fundamental mind" is interchangeable with other terms such as "Buddha-nature," "true nature," "true self," and "foundation."

least in part through this fundamental mind. Many scientists and researchers already understand this, if only half-consciously. They use their intellect and knowledge, of course, but they also put that to work through their fundamental mind.

In this way they've been able to create all kinds of new materials and technology that we now find indispensable. Starting with earth, water, fire, and air, scientists developed the ideas and theories that led to further developments, like lasers and such.

"Laser," somebody sure came up with a good name. Those are used everywhere, aren't they? In hospitals, planes, satellites, radio, TV, phones – lasers have become indispensable in our lives. They can be used across vast distances, as well as very close distances.

Although all of their uses are amazing, let's look at what's possible through spiritual practice and *relying upon our fundamental mind.*[8] We can go to the past and return, we can go to the future, and any kind of karma can be melted down. Problems caused by *samsara,*[9] genetics, ghosts, germs, and karma can all be dissolved and changed into something positive. Not only this.

***

8. Relying upon our fundamental mind: Trusting and relying upon our fundamental mind is the essence of spiritual practice and growth in all Daehaeng Kun Sunim's teachings. It's the foundation of all spiritual progress. We all have this Buddha-nature, this original face, this inherent mind, and, in fact, everything in our life revolves around it.

When teaching people about spiritual practice, Daehaeng Kun Sunim always emphasized that the very first step was just being aware that we all have this inherent nature. The next step was trying to rely upon it. This means taking what's confronting us, what's arising in our life, and doing our best to entrust that to this fundamental essence and then to let go of it. As we entrust something, we let go of it and just be aware, observing what's going on, without trying to watch too closely and see what happens.

As we keep working at this, we'll get experiences, times when everything seems to just click into place. We will experience times when we truly let go unconditionally, without a lot of "I" or "me," letting this inherent Buddha-nature take care of what we entrusted. As we see it working, as we experience this for ourselves, our faith in it naturally becomes deeper, and we are better able to entrust more and more. This practice of relying upon our fundamental mind, our Buddha-nature, is a self-correcting path that seems narrow in the beginning, but which eventually becomes a great highway.

9. Samsara: The endless cycle of birth and death that all living things are continuously passing through.

If, for example, there are ten thousand people, then through this practice, you can become those ten thousand people, and they can become you. In the face of this practice, numbers have no meaning. Buddha can become one with anything, and manifest and respond to it all. In the midst of this, how could there be any separation between you and me?

Through knowing and relying upon our foundation we can be utterly free of all hindrances, have the ability to help with whatever is needed, be able to transcend time, and able to finally dissolve all of our old karma as it continuously comes out in our lives. In so doing we can even change our future.

Regardless of whether something is near or far, if you want to see it, then you'll see it as if it was brought before you. If you want to examine it, then you'll see it down to the smallest aspect. If you need something, you'll be able to bring it forth and use it, and if something is needed elsewhere, you'll be able to bring that forth too and give it. Through this practice, you do all of this freely, as needed.

If you want the birds of the air to land on the ground, then they will, and if you want to stop a missile from flying up into the sky, this too will happen. Knowing and connecting with this foundation of ours is just so incredible – how can I describe it all? The ability and authority that this practice bestows is inconceivable. It's like being given the authority to take care of anything in the *universe.*[10]

Even now, I'm only talking about the things that people can easily understand and follow. Sakyamuni Buddha too, taught people according to their ability to understand. To those of great capacity, he taught much. To those of more limited capacity, he taught only a little, in a way that they could understand. Because that was all they could absorb.

For this is something that can only be learned through practice, right where we are. Other people's words, theories, or intellectual learning

---

10. Universe: This includes all visible realms, as well as all unseen realms.

can't take the place of our own experience and knowledge. Old, young, male, female, noble, lowly, whoever, we can only truly understand the essence of what the Buddha spoke of through this practice of relying upon our fundamental *mind*.[11]

When Sakyamuni declared that the layman *Vimalakirti*[12] was his own *Dharma brother*,[13] it was to make it clear that this practice was available to anyone and everyone.

---

11. Mind(心)(Korean – *maum*)**:** In Mahayana Buddhism, "mind" refers to this fundamental mind, and almost never means the brain or intellect. It is intangible, beyond space and time, and has no beginning or end. It is the source of everything, and everyone is endowed with it.

12. Vimalakirti: A lay disciple of Sakyamuni Buddha who was renowned for the depth of his enlightenment. His name means "Pure" or "Unstained." He appears in the Vimalakirti-Nirdesa Sutra, where he taught even the great disciples of the Buddha. He is portrayed as the ideal layperson, one who attained the essence of the Buddha-dharma and who thoroughly applied his understanding to his life. He would help those who were poor and suffering, and teach and educate those who were behaving badly.

13. Dharma brother: A fellow practitioner. There is also a strong nuance of recognition of Vimalakirti as someone of impressive spiritual depth and standing.

Please think about this. From the perspective of the Earth, human beings are just another animal, and often act no better than animals. Nonetheless, they have a sense of the preciousness of all life, and often work to protect it all.

Yet from microbes all the way to humans, everyone has been killing and eating each other, or being killed and eaten. It seems like just endless pain and war on an unimaginable scale. It's so vicious. Battles are happening all the time where neither sword nor gun is drawn. Now, having made it through all of this pain and suffering, stop acting like someone stuck in those lower levels! Right here, start seeing the world from a higher, broader perspective. See how things look.

People are being chased, even though no one is chasing them, and are being hunted and eaten, even as they hunt and eat others. This is the world we are living in. You may be completely healthy, yet suddenly become disabled without even knowing why. Or you could be suddenly struck down by a mental disability. Sometimes, seeing people go through this again and again, without ever trying to escape from it, gets too much for me, and I can only look at the heavens and sigh.

Everything in the world is connected and tied together, but people don't know this, and instead put all their focus on "my body," "my family." They don't learn to see the larger context, and end up unable to see what's coming towards them, even when it's only an inch away.

Not seeing any farther, they don't know what they should truly be doing, nor how to find a way forward. What I see what people go through… [Sighs.] If they'd just throw everything away, and keep doing that, then even though they lived like some kind of gentle fool, they could stop hunting and killing each other. They wouldn't be chasing and biting each other like two rats trapped in a bucket.

Sometimes people think that Buddhism is going to the temple and expecting that the Buddha will save them, but it's not. Sakyamuni Buddha told everyone very clearly "Know yourself." He said to them, "Do you think my body is any different from yours? Do you really think that my mind is any different? Both are exactly the same as yours. The only difference is in the kind of thoughts I give rise to."

Everywhere you go in the world you'll find some form of religion, won't you? Catholicism, Protestantism, Buddhism, Islam, and they all have their own beliefs and faith. Yet if you look closely at how people are behaving, they are trying to convince some outer power to give them what they want. They obscure their own inner eye, and end up unable to see even an inch in front of themselves. They are clueless about what's happening to them, and clueless about what's developing in front of them.

If you put all your faith in others, and ignore what you already have within, then for life after life you will be no more than a slave. Do you really want to live as a poor sharecropper?

The Buddha did not teach people to become beggars. He taught how to walk the Earth with dignity. Don't be lame, don't be blind, and don't be deaf. Know that all of the universe, all of the great Dharma realms, and all of their power, ability, and energy are directly connected to your mind. This is what he taught!

Whenever the layman Vimalakirti met monks who were focused on sitting meditation, he would ask them, "What happens when you stand up? Doesn't your practice then come to an end? He would counsel them, and teach them like this so that they could find their own way forward.

He also said, "My body will become healthy only after all unenlightened beings become healthy." People often misunderstand this and think that he meant that he had to save all of the beings outside his body in order for his own illness to be healed.

But it's the lives within the body that have to be saved in order for the body to be healed. If their consciousnesses can be raised so that they work together harmoniously, then as those lives begin to function properly, the body as a whole will be healed.

We need to teach those lives within us, those consciousnesses, that they do not exist apart from each other. It's through this fundamental mind of ours that we can teach them that we are all part of the same whole. This is how we have to guide all of the unenlightened beings that make up our body.

We, as individuals, have no sense of where the Earth is going, do we? Just like this, the lives that make up our organs, flesh, and bones have no idea if this body is headed towards Busan or Seoul. It's up to us to communicate with them and let them know what's going on. Only then, can all the consciousnesses of the lives within us fully work together, and respond as one to our intentions. Then we can bring in whatever is needed and send out what needs to be sent out, and function with complete freedom, manifesting in a million different ways, according to the need.

Let me put it this way: You have to be able to get all of these billions of consciousnesses within you to respond to and follow your words and intentions. You do this by gathering them together in your *one mind*,[14] and then you keep doing this. You have to keep doing this. Then they'll begin to follow your intentions. You have to develop this kind of spiritual ability.

But so many people don't realize that each of us has this fundamental mind, and so they don't try to make it their center, and because there is no center, the consciousnesses of the lives within wander off on their own. If we don't try to rely upon our fundamental mind, this true essence, and entrust it with everything we face, then all the parts of our body will function as if they were isolated from the whole. The stomach would do its own thing, the intestines, the bladder, the spine, the kidneys, and so on, would all act without understanding their part in the whole.

14. One mind (*Hanmaum* [han-ma-um]): From the Korean, where "one" has a nuance of great and combined, while "mind" is more than intellect and includes "heart" as well. Together, they mean everything combined and connected as one. What is called "one mind" is intangible, unseen, and transcends time and space. It has no beginning or end, and is sometimes called our fundamental mind. It also means the mind of all beings and everything in the universe connected and working together as one.

It's like the old saying, "If there's no tiger on the mountain, the foxes run around thinking each is the lord of creation." It's like each part of the body thinks it alone is the boss, and so won't follow any other part. And it won't follow your intentions. How then could you respond when the truly hard parts of life arise?

This mind has no form or color or fixed shape. It embraces the entire universe and all lives within, freely functioning and taking care of everything, using power and ability beyond imagining. It can do all of this exactly because it is not some limited, material thing.

When you're looking at all aspects of a thing, and decide what's needed, this mind races forward to take care of it. Faster than even a laser beam. You can use the ability of your mind to take care of anything in the universe, but, frankly, often times people use it only for such small, petty things that it's a bit like children showing off their toys.

Even though I tell people all about how this works, they're still so quick to believe in others, and so reluctant to believe in their own essence. I'll bet this has frustrated everyone who's ever awakened. Even though everyone has this great power within themselves to affect the world around them, they refuse to trust this. They could rule over everything in the universe if they would just trust this ability.

I used the words, "rule over," didn't I? But when I say "rule over" or "govern the entire universe," I don't mean doing this from some high ranking position and forcing everything to do what you want. Instead, I mean that if you meet fire, then you become one with it. When you meet air, you become one with it, and meeting the earth, you become one with it. Encountering unseen spirits of the dead, you become one with them. Meeting living people, you become one with them. Only when you can truly become one with whatever you meet, will you be able to take care of anything that arises.

So then, what of the lives that make up our very own body? Shouldn't we also become one with them? You are completely capable of this. Never doubt that you can become one with all these lives inside you. Even though a single twig seems weak and insignificant, if you gather a bunch of them together into a bundle, they become unbreakable, don't they? Now think about all the billions of lives within our bodies. Although each is tiny and fragile, if they all function together as one, nothing can overcome them. So having faith that you can gather all of these lives together is where you have to start.

There are some people who turn their back on *Juingong*[15] when they don't immediately get better after trying to entrust their illness. They try for a little bit but then give up. Because they give up so easily, nothing has a chance to develop. But when a problem is being caused by a giant pile of karmic

---

15. Juingong (主人空, [Ju-in-gong]): Pronounced "ju-in-gong." *Juin*(主人) means the true doer or the master, and *gong*(空) means empty. Thus, Juingong is our true nature, our true essence, the master within that is always changing and manifesting, with no fixed form or shape.

Daehaeng Sunim has compared Juingong to the root of the tree. Our bodies and consciousness are like the branches and leaves, but it is the root that is the source of the tree, and it is the root that sustains the visible tree.

consciousnesses, do you think that just letting go once or twice will be enough?

Let me tell you a story about something that happened a long time ago, when a woman from Chungju visited me in tears. She had been ill for some time and finally came up to Seoul to see a specialist, who diagnosed her with leukemia. Because she'd been sick, she hadn't been able to do much housework, and had spent a lot of money on doctors, so her husband was giving her a hard time.

As she cried, she gave an offering of a bag of rice, some candles, and 250,000 won. Let's see, Mrs. Lee So Jeo still ran her inn in Seoul, so it would have been about 1970. Which was a lot of money for those days.[16]

Back then, I didn't teach people about relying upon their fundamental mind the way that I do now. She was crying and in pain, but didn't know

---

16. This would have been a bit over US $5,000 in 2015 dollars. Mrs. Lee So Jeo would later donate the land for the Anyang Hanmaum Seon Center.

anything about how to take her suffering and entrust it to her foundation. She was in so much pain that she couldn't even think about anything else, so I just took care of the outer problem that her karmic consciousnesses were causing. Once the pain was gone, she could hear what I had to say to her.

The lady stayed at Mrs. Lee's inn for several days, and went to see her doctor for another exam. As he looked at her results, he said there must have been a mistake before, because now she had no trace of leukemia. When her husband heard this, he was furious and accused her of wasting his money. He came up to Seoul and demanded the money, so I just gave it back.

Prior to this, I had told Mrs. Lee to just leave it there, wrapped up just as the lady had brought it. Mrs. Lee suggested using the rice to feed visitors, but I told her that someone would soon be coming for it.

As I had anticipated, he came demanding the money, ready to start throwing his fists around. So I just gave it to him, of course. It was like a child who eats an ice cream and then demands his money back because now he doesn't have any ice cream. What can you do but shake your head?

How could you come demanding offerings made to the Buddha? Of course, if he could have understood this point, he wouldn't have behaved like that in the first place. Although his wife recovered and was fine, he later ended up coming down with cancer. For when he took back her offering, he also took with him all the unseen causes of her illness.

As I've said before, it's the functioning of karmic states of consciousness that causes these kinds of things. These karmic consciousnesses…, you have to dissolve them yourself, through your foundation. Otherwise, they'll always hunt you down. Even if you take care of one aspect, they just pop up later with a different form. These karmic states are woven throughout all your relationships and history, so there's not just one cause for what you're experiencing. Anyway, the poor man was so ashamed of how he behaved that he never did come see me again, even when he was sick.

A while later a friend of the couple happened to visit me. During our conversation, she said, "You've helped them so much in the past, can't you do something now? When she had severe depression, you helped her. When she couldn't get pregnant, you helped her. And when she came down with leukemia, you helped her. Can't you do something for her husband now?"

My first thought was, "There's nothing more I can do for him." But he was in so much pain, so I told her that if he couldn't keep anything else down, then drinking potato juice everyday might help him. Does that sound like some special medicine? No. But with it, I entrusted the thought that he should recover. And the last I heard, he's still alive. In any event, no matter how badly someone else behaves, no matter what suffering they cause you, never, ever raise a thought that they should suffer or come to harm.

Only when you let go of even whether you live or die, will true faith arise. Only then will you begin to know unwavering faith in your foundation. This fundamental mind of yours existed trillions of years ago, it formed you from microbes, and even as you passed through an endless cycle of eating and being eaten, it helped you evolve to where you are now. Yet people go through life not trusting this foundation. This foundation that's been guiding them all this time.

If you give in to fears about death and desperately try to cling to life, then even after you die, even though you've entered the process of dying and being reborn, you'll still have a hard time evolving. So have faith in your inner Buddha, your foundation, and completely entrust it with everything.

Flip flopping around isn't faith. This foundation has given rise to you, so know that it can also take care of you, and go forward. For illness of the mind, cure them through mind, for problems of the flesh, take care of your body and make wise use of doctors and hospitals. If you entrust everything – the pain, the illness, the doctor who wants to treat you – to your Juingong, then energy and understanding will flow back and forth between your foundation and the people treating you. And so, your treatment will go much smoother.

Using the material aspect to take care of things is also important. This world and ourselves are composed of every kind of matter and energy, and through this, the intentions arising from our fundamental mind spread out like a wave and manifest into the world. This transmission is so fast, there's no gap between sending and receiving.

When we raise an intention from our foundation, the energy that comes from this is so powerful, it's like there is a massive power plant within us generating it. Like energy sent out along power lines, or radio and TV waves showing up in our homes, when we raise a thought from our foundation, it goes out through our brain to all the parts of our body, communicating with them all.

In this way, all these lives that make up our body can function together as one, according to the intention we give rise to. Further, because neither the mind nor consciousnesses of these lives have physical form, they can freely go back and forth from our body, examining the situation around us and taking care of it. If all the lives within us become one like this, then each understands that, "I am Buddha. I am all unenlightened beings. And so, I need to take care of them all."

A high school boy who comes to the Seon center had an experience like this not too long ago. He was taking a shortcut through a back street when some older boys suddenly pulled knives on him and demanded all his money. He was so surprised and shocked that he just stood there, frozen. But he thought about what he'd heard here, and silently, sincerely, called out, "Juingong! Kun Sunim!" because he was so desperate. They turned his pockets inside out, but all he had with him was 10,000 won (about US $10). Instead of beating him up, they just swore at him and left.

He told me that until then he'd just followed his parents to the Seon center, and had never practiced entrusting anything. All he'd done was listen to my talk about entrusting until that moment when he was desperate. The urgency of the situation focused him on entrusting that confrontation to Juingong.

So the consciousnesses of the lives that make up his body all became one, and were focused on protecting him. They went and changed the vicious intentions of those young men into a kinder state, so that they just left the boy there, without hurting him. Now he understands the power of entrusting!

You need this kind of unconditional trust in this inherent Buddha essence of yours. This has to underlie everything else. Yet so many people get caught up in trying to accumulate knowledge – memorizing the sutras, studying others' theories, cleverly dissecting out different points, and so on. They end up thinking they know something, but all they've done is make everything fit the framework of their own fixed ideas. Despite how clever they appear, people like this have a hard time actually developing deep faith in their foundation.

This is why Sakyamuni Buddha said that those people without much education or cleverness are often able to have much deeper faith in their foundation, and so make more progress in their practice. Sometimes people with a lot of knowledge tend to get caught up in scepticism, and are suspicious of everything. But what is there to doubt when it comes to believing in what you truly are?

If I was telling you to believe in someone else, or to believe in their power, then you might want to step carefully. But I'm not. I'm telling you to believe in your own foundation, your fundamental essence, which has been leading you forward for eons. I'm not telling to rely on other's flesh nor to put your faith in lofty titles, nor to believe in some place up in the sky. Your inherent nature is what led you to be born into this world, and through which you perceive and experience everything. So trust this. Regardless of where you are in your life, of how things are going, trust your true self.

This is why I'm always saying that you have to know your foundation, what you truly are. However, sometimes people treat sitting meditation as if it was some inherent, unique truth that could awaken them to the *Buddha-dharma*,[17] but this isn't the case. Everything you encounter, everything you go through each day, all of the living and dying, is Buddhism in its entirety. It is the Buddha-dharma, meditation, kong-ans, and *true suchness*.[18] Know this: It is through all the things and experiences of your daily life that awakening can be found.

In the word "Juingong," the character for "gong (空)" means "*emptiness.*"[19] Because everything in this world is constantly changing and flowing, with nothing that remains stationary. Nothing!

---

17. Buddha-dharma: This can refer to the fundamental reality that the teachings of Buddha point towards, or, occasionally, the teachings themselves.

18. True suchness: Here, Daehaeng Kun Sunim is saying that everything we encounter in our daily lives is the teachings of the truth (the Buddha-dharma), a method for awakening to the truth (such as meditation and kong-ans,) and the state of being one with the truth (true suchness.)

Do your eyes see only the same, one image? Do you hear only the same sound? What you see and hear constantly changes, doesn't it? You hear one thing, then another, and then something else. And your thoughts and feelings change accordingly. Instantly going to the past, the future, and every kind of place.

This continuous flowing of the whole, of everything, is itself meditation, true suchness, Buddhism, and is the true meaning of religion. All of this is right here, in every part of your life. When you try to live like this, then you will come to know your true nature – your true essence – and see that it's leading you forward every moment. You will begin to realize that this foundation is what causes you to exist, what lets you die, and what lets you

---

19. Emptiness: Emptiness is not a void, but rather refers to the ceaseless flowing of all things. Everything is flowing as part of one whole, so there is nothing that can be separated out and set aside as if it existed independently of everything else. There is, therefore, no "me" that exists apart from other people or other things. There is only the interpenetrated and interdependent whole, "empty" of any independent or separate selves or objects.

take shape again. What else is there that you think someone else can do for you? There, in the midst of living, of becoming, and disappearing, all is done by mind. [Holding up one finger.]

No matter how hard we worked to be born as a human being, no matter how diligently we live, all it takes is one illness, and everything's over. It takes so little to bring this human life to an end. It's so tenuous. What do the mountains and great trees think about us as we pass by? Walking through the forests and twelve thousand peaks of the Diamond Mountains, we must seem to them like mayflies. If all you know is this material flesh, then this certainly seems to be the case.

Someone I was talking with gave a sigh and said it was such a shame that her grandparents and great-grandparents never got to experience life in the country that Korea has become. These days, everything is so developed and prosperous, but they all lived and died during such hard times. However, our ancestors aren't frozen in the past. They're already here, now, living with us in this same world.

Just as the Diamond Mountains reverberate with the energy and stories of their thousand hermitages, we have right here within us, everything that we have experienced and undergone. Even though our lives seem fragile and short, we carry everything we've done with us. All of the past, present, and even the future are right here, right now.

Everything that happened in the past is also happening right now, and everything that will happen in the future is also being created right now. We are living here in this present life together with all the past, present, and future.

If you really want to become spiritually free, if you want to know how to grow and live as a true human being, then start with faith in your inherent essence. Right here, now, in your day-to-day life, diligently and honestly work at trusting this essence with whatever is going on. So that even if you were about to die, you wouldn't blink an eye. "Okay, true nature, you formed me, so if this existence is finished, then let's be done with it. If I need to continue this longer, then let's do that. You figure it out!" Even though you let go of everything like this, you won't go wrong.

At any rate, either way we are all going to die, so before that time comes, why not try to experiment with having this kind of trust in our essence? See what happens when you start living like this.

By trusting your inherent Buddha-nature with all that you're going through, the lives within your body will all begin function together as one, following the lead of your Buddha-nature. How could they not become healthy and joyous? If you can evolve like this during this life, how could you not come out at a higher level in your next life? How could you not be born with deeper wisdom and insight?

To be perfectly frank, it is an incredible thing to learn to rely upon this fundamental essence and apply its energy to the world around us. For without doing this, you may never taste or experience this treasure that each of us has. I suspect that awakened beings have always felt frustrated as they observed the speech and actions of people who were ignorant of this treasure. Yet what could they do? No one else can do this for you. You have to want it and work for it yourself.

This is why some Seon masters just ignored the world, and lived free and easy. [Laughs.] They must have thought to themselves, "Empty tin cans bang together and make all kinds of noise. And gold gathers together with gold and shines even brighter. They will live as they will. Ho! What can someone else do about it?" This *middle world*[20] we are now living in is like a sieve, sifting people into higher or lower realms, according to how they live.

As I mentioned in the last talk, there isn't some separate place called Hell. Let me try to explain this for a bit. If you live this life like a poisonous snake, then after death that's the kind of body you will

---

20. Middle world: In Buddhism, the realm of human beings is sometimes described as the "middle realm" or the "middle world," because it said to be one of six realms. It exists below the realms of more advanced beings, called devas and asuras, but above the realms of animals, hungry ghosts, and the various hell states.

be drawn towards. This is the invisible, automatic process of cause and effect, and *karmic affinity*,[21] and is truly fearsome.

Imagine someone who is reborn as a snake. They will have all the habits and some of the consciousness of a human being. Yet they'll be trapped in a snake's body, with all its limitations. That right there is hell.

A long time ago, I happened to see a shaman performing an exorcism. She was dancing with a sword, waving it around and scattering bits of porridge around the yard. All the while, she was shouting, "Go away! If you don't leave now, you'll never again smell steamed rice or soup!" This meant that if that ghost didn't stop bothering the person it was inhabiting, then it's harmful behavior would cause it to be reborn at some low level like that of a burrowing insect, where it would be beyond contact with human beings.

---

21. Karmic affinity(因緣)**:** The connection or attraction between people or things, due to previous karmic relationships.

Although the shaman herself didn't know the implications of what she was saying, in any event, it's true that someone who lives like an animal or insect will next take the body of an animal or insect. Both heaven and hell are right here, where we are living now.

Look at yourself for a moment. A human being is so impressive! Everything is there, including even what are called the *five subtle powers*.[22] These have all the capabilities of cameras, mobile phones, radars, and telescopes. They make it possible to see anything, to hear anything, to know others' minds, to know the past and future, and to go anywhere without moving your body. These abilities all arise from your fundamental mind, automatically communicating and bringing things together. They catch everything, so if you yell at someone or give

---

22. Five subtle powers (五神通)**:** The power to know past and future lives, the power to know others' thoughts and emotions, the power to see anything, the power to hear anything, and the power to go anywhere.

them a hard time, that's input, and in time will cause you to create situations where you end up being yelled at.

So, as best you can, entrust everything to your essence, Juingong. It's what is doing everything; do you think your flesh is just moving around on its own? What you see on the TV isn't being made by that square box. It's a fragile thing that becomes useless if just one bit of wiring or cable is cut. Further, you're the one who makes the decisions about what that TV displays. You're the one who decides what will be seen or not seen; the TV doesn't just do that on its own. It's not the shell you should trust, but rather the essence that moves it.

All the parts of our body, all of our organs, all of our flesh, all the lives and consciousnesses that make up this body all follow this one mind. They all respond to one mind. So, if we don't truly know what's going on, if we're being swept up by circumstances, then shouldn't we be placing our trust in this foundation that has guided us this far?

Right now, our home, this earth, the solar system, and the galaxy, are all hurtling through space. Does anyone here know where we're headed? Can that ever be known by anyone?

A member of the audience   Ah, but isn't knowing what we don't know also knowing? [Kun Sunim and the audience laugh.]

Kun Sunim   No, it pretty much just means that you don't know. [Laughs.] It's like the cells that make up this body of ours. They have no idea where the body is going or what it's doing. So, if you let them know that they and all the other cells are actually one whole body – if through your foundation, you make these consciousnesses one with you – then one part won't end up hurting another part. They'll understand that, "All of this is me!"

So, have unconditional faith in your own foundation! Whether an illness improves, or doesn't, whether things start going the way you want, or don't, trust that in all of this, your foundation is leading you forward. It guided you through billions of years, helping you evolve into a human being while you've hunted and been hunted, pushing you to grow and change. And now, although you've been born as a human, you still haven't reached the end. Now you have to take the things banging into you and use them to evolve your mind.

So, no matter what kind of hardship you encounter, take it as something to practice with. Even if the world were to end right now, even though you're scared and panicky, have firm trust in your foundation. If you can watch it happen and laughingly say, "What, again?" if your faith is this deep and calm, then you'll be able to manage whatever happens and guide it in a better direction. You absolutely must have faith in this essence that's been guiding you. To not have trust in it is like abandoning yourself.

You have to believe in this divine essence that exists within you. Could you really not trust this?

It's what is animating you right now. What else, where else would you rely upon? Is there anyone else who can take your place when you fall ill? Is there anything else who can stand in for you when death comes? No. No matter how much your children love you, no matter how much your wife or husband cares for you, no one can even stand in for you when you need to use the toilet. No one can take your place when you need sleep, or are sick, or are dying.

Rely upon and trust your inherent essence. Go forward trusting this essence that has lead you across a billion eons, and worked to evolve you. If you have steadfast faith in this and entrust it with everything you experience, then your mind will rapidly evolve and the wisdom and ability you develop will cause your family to live together joyfully. Doing all this is the essence of all the Buddha's teachings.

Now, are there any questions today?

Questioner 1 (Male) I'd like to ask you about the role of science and its relationship with cause and effect. This is something I've wondered about for a while now. Science has been revealing the secrets of DNA bit by bit, and recent journal articles reported that a French team has uncovered an aspect of genes that they believe will be the key to treating genetic diseases. They report that within the next twenty years or so, this will make it possible for us to treat thousands of previously incurable genetic diseases.

If this is true, then I have a question. As I understand it, genetic diseases and incurable diseases are the accumulated results of what we've done over the eons. Is there really a way for science to overcome these results of cause and effect?

It seems that if science can fix this through an understanding of genetics, then it can subsume this unseen realm of mind and the results of that energy. If so, it seems like a new understanding of cause and effect is necessary.

Kun Sunim No matter how wondrous a treatment scientists have discovered, it is still only dealing with the physical, material issues that are presenting at that moment in time. But those doctors don't truly know why or how that genetic disease arose, nor all of the things connected with it. So even if they think they cured it, the underlying issues still haven't been eliminated. In the case of problems caused by karma, they will reappear as a new kind of suffering, with different names.

Thus, you have to return to your fundamental mind and dissolve those causes there. If you want to truly erase data, you record something new over the top of it, right? Otherwise, there's still something left behind. And that won't just disappear on its own.

This is why I always say, "You have to let go of everything to your fundamental mind." Then, once you know your fundamental mind, your true self, you'll see how it functions as one with everything. If you become one with the sun, you will see things from the perspective of the sun, and will truly understand the mechanics and functioning of the rest of the solar system.

Yet if you don't know where a disease came from, if you don't truly know the conditions that caused it to arise, then even though you come up with a theory or treatment for it, you won't be able to truly cure it.

Let me give you an example. When farmers have problems with insects destroying their crops, they spray them with pesticides. At first this kills off the bugs. However, those bugs know what hurt them, so they try to think about how they can survive. With that intention, they begin to change and are reborn with an altered form, and so those pesticides become less and less effective.

Karma, genetics, microbes, ghosts and such can cause people to become confused, or to lose their faith. To say nothing of their influence on all kinds of other things in a person's life. Similarly, there are all kinds of new names of diseases, names that fill people with fear. Names that didn't exist in the past, such as leukemia, bone marrow cancer, and so on. If you can gather your strength and kick out the fear and confusion these inspire, entrusting the situation to your foundation, it will likely disappear.

All those names are just letters of the alphabet. If, through your fundamental mind, you can encompass all the lives in your body, such that they all work together as one, then "cancer," or whatever, just becomes empty letters. Just like you go to the toilet when you feel pressure in your bowels, the cells and lives in your body will respond to what's going on, and work all together, naturally, to take care of it.

Questioner 2 (Male)   Although this is supposedly the era of cutting edge science, there are still so many diseases doctors can't cure, nor even alleviate. Yet, to my surprise, I've seen diseases like these disappear almost magically when people began to apply your teachings.

Of course, I suspect the spiritual power arising from your own practice played a role, but I was wondering if you could tell us the secret by which these people were cured. And, um, since I'm here, could you please embrace all of us with your spiritual power so that we may always practice without being distracted by disease?

Kun Sunim   [Laughs.] As I've always told you, it's neither me nor you who cures the disease. If it can be said to be anything, it is this nondual mind, flowing back and forth. It's like the lights coming on when electricity flows through the whole that the light bulbs, wiring and switch. There's no "me" that cures, nor is there a "you" who recovers. In the midst of this combined whole, there is only light that becomes brighter.

This is how you have to practice. Only then can you complete yourself. Only then can you realize the potential of this incredibly close, friendly Buddha you all have within you.

Questioner 2   Since we're on the topic of disease, about six or seven years ago my legs started getting weaker and weaker. Further, my big toenails would break off as they grew out. I have no idea why this happened. However, around the beginning of this year, I started to see some changes. Now instead of breaking off, my toenails are growing out properly. I still have some discomfort, but, they're much better than before. I guess this means the rest of my body is improving as well?

Kun Sunim [Laughs.] Of course, of course! This practice of relying upon and discovering our fundamental essence is so amazing! This practice is such a wondrous thing, with so much potential. Thus the Buddha said, "Even when this flesh of mine no longer exists, if you exist, I will be there with you, regardless of the era. So be diligent and awaken to the realm of no-self."

All the lives within your body have their own respective consciousness, and each was recorded, each was created, according to how we were living at that moment in time. And then they come back out according to circumstances and fill our awareness. So, for no reason at all, you may suddenly feel the desire to steal something, or to deceive someone, or to do something nice, and so forth.

Yet beneath all of these is something that is able to know what is truly good, what is bad, and what will make things go better or worse. We have to make this essence the captain of our ship, so that it's able to manage and take care of everything we encounter.

We can make this happen by returning everything back place it came from. If you return it all inwardly, those karmic states of consciousness become one with this captain, your fundamental mind. They become one, and so the captain can communicate with them. Because the captain is communicating with them, they follow the captain. As these consciousnesses of the lives within you begin to follow the captain, the parts of your body that were weak become stronger, and parts that were too strong begin to settle down. So, as you keep returning everything, your body will naturally become healthier.

Years ago in Korea, there were many people who suffered from polio or encephalitis. At that time the son of a member here came down with one of those. So I taught him and his mother this, and both practiced diligently. His legs were painfully thin, but gradually they filled out and became quite strong. He grew into a healthy adult, and got a job at a big company, and now lives quite well.

There are many people here who have had similar experiences. When others can grow and live well like this, it makes me so happy! They too, are happy, and the ability they develop to trust in their foundation will bring them blessings for life after life. Take other's successful examples and use those to improve your own practice and deepen yourself.

You've learned that there is this captain, that it exists within you, and that all the lives and consciousnesses that make up your body will follow the thoughts of this captain, so, if you keep working on entrusting everything you feel and are going through to this captain, those lives responsible for that will surrender and follow the captain.

To explain "surrender" another way, all of those lives will become one with the captain, your fundamental Buddha essence. If you keep surrendering those consciousnesses to your captain, then later because they all become one, you'll find that there was nothing that surrendered, and nothing that accepted the surrender. There is only suchness, where all things are complete just as they are.

That said, be patient even when it seems like your progress is slow. Don't get caught up in comparing yourself to others or wondering why you can't do the same things they can. Just keep working at your own practice with a firm resolution. As you do this, you'll experience things you've only heard about, such as seeing auras, hearing things from faraway, or being able to leave your body and go somewhere else.

When you experience these things, be sure to let go and entrust them to your foundation. Be grateful, and know that those experiences are there to teach you, but, nonetheless, return them inwardly. You must not cling to those or try to cultivate them. You have to be free from even the five subtle powers.

Think of this cup [holding up a cup of water] as the five subtle powers. If you want to lift it up, if you want to drink from it, you have to be outside of it, don't you? If you were in the cup, you couldn't do anything with it.

To put it another way, the five subtle powers are not the far shore of enlightenment. They exist only on this side of the river, within the realms of *ignorance*.[23] Achieving them is not enlightenment. Once we cross over to the far shore, then we can use these and anything else we need as we respond to and take care of the entire universe.

---

23. Ignorance (無明)**:** In Buddhism, "ignorance" literally means darkness. It is the unenlightened mind that does not see the truth. It is being unaware of the inherent oneness of all things, and it is the fundamental cause of birth, aging, sickness, and death.

When I think of everything that's possible through this practice of working through our fundamental essence, it's just so incredible and powerful! Most ordinary people can't even conceive of its potential, let alone try to practice it like you all are. In the past, only those who cut off all attachments and became monks or nuns could learn this. However, if you understand what the Buddha spent forty-nine years teaching, if you understand the meaning of why the Buddha and Vimalakirti worked together to guide unenlightened beings to freedom, then you're fully capable of doing this practice.

Vimalakirti, too, appeared in this world in order to show ordinary people that they too can practice and awaken.

When he said "I will become well only after all those beings suffering illness have been cured," people often misunderstood this to mean all beings throughout the universe. However, what he meant is that you have to save the unenlightened beings within you. When these lives within you become strong and robust, then won't your whole body become healthy?

That said, there's Korean saying that if you hit the wall, the rafters should shake. There are two implications here. First, you should make such effort that even the rafters shake, and second, don't lose sight of the larger goal.

Questioner 2   Thank you, I'll keep working hard.

Kun Sunim   I truly appreciate your efforts. If your legs become strong and you can walk uprightly through this world, what could be better?

Questioner 3 (Male)   Hello, I'm a psychiatrist, and a member of the Seon center's science group. I'd like to ask you about how to treat mental illnesses, and schizophrenia in particular.

Among the severe disorders, schizophrenia affects the most people and is one of the most difficult to treat. It's usually what people are seeing when they encounter a "crazy" person, and it affects about one percent of the population. Patients can suffer from auditory and visual hallucinations, and the onset can be sudden or gradual. It completely disrupts their lives, and as it progresses, it often leaves them unable to function in society.

Although doctors know about the symptoms in detail, we have only guesses as to its causes. There are a couple of different medicines that can treat the symptoms, but patients have to take them for the rest of their lives, and they can cause extreme mental fuzziness, and any number of other very unpleasant side effects.

When patients take these for ten or twenty years, they start losing interest in the world around them, almost as if they are losing their desire to live, and have a hard time handling the basics of daily life.

As a doctor, I know that these medicines are the only thing that seems to help this disease, and so I prescribe them and urge my patients to take them. But I myself am uneasy about these drugs.

I've agonized over this for many years, wondering what the best course might be, and if there isn't a better way to treat patients with schizophrenia. I would like to ask you for anything that I and my fellow doctors can use to help people suffering from this disease.

Kun Sunim   This kind of disease can arise from three possible directions. It could be caused by something about the patients themselves, it could be caused by an outside influence, or it could be the results of something their ancestors did.

But to doctors, the symptoms all look the same, so they try to treat each patient in the same way. They give all their patients the same medicine, but it only works for some patients, while causing even more problems for other patients. Thus, doctors and patients need to look beyond just those medicines. The patient's parents, family, and those around them, to say nothing of their doctors, should learn about how to rely upon this fundamental mind.

If they are all working on connecting with this, if they are all inputting the intention that the patient should recover and be able to function and think clearly, then the energy of that will help the patient, who then may be able to recover much easier than expected. When thoroughly entrusted, those intentions can function at the unseen level, where all beings are connected.

In cases where the schizophrenia is quite severe, you may have to also hospitalize those patients, but everything I just said still applies.

However, if people don't know about this, and just keep giving the patient drugs, then over time their body functions will begin to deteriorate. They begin to lose their vividness, their courage, and their will to live. Finally, even thinking becomes difficult. Their body still lives, so they move about, but what kind of life is this? What's happened to all of the potential they were born with?

So, try to avoid long term use of medicines that will cause their minds to deteriorate. Instead, give them courage, let them know that it is their mind, their foundation that moves and takes care of their body. If they can know this, and begin to trust it, then their illness will start to fade. [To the audience:] Everyone, if you know someone who's suffering from this type of mental illness, raise and entrust this same intention on their behalf.

Recently, I visited a prison in Chicago that housed the most violent offenders. They had a large room where they kept prisoners with severe mental illness, who were too disruptive for the regular prison. I asked the person in charge to put a large sign on the wall, saying "Hey! True self! You're the one that can take care of this!" In addition I stationed several good spirits there to help them. With those invisible hands helping, about half the people there should become better. So, since patients like this are your specialty as well, why don't you give this a try! [Smiles.]

Questioner 3 Okay, I'll work hard at doing you've said.

Questioner 4 (female) I came here today to express my deep appreciation for your teachings. I'd been going through a rough time, struggling with despair and confusion, when a cousin gave me your books *Mu* (Nothing) and *Do* (The Path). As I read them, I began to sense something deeper, but although I wanted to find this true mind, I couldn't. I began to realize that I needed to let go of the persistent thoughts of "I" and "me," but I couldn't seem to make much progress with this.

I began to think that it would help if I could meet you in person, and so I came to see you about a year ago. Although it was wonderful, my behavior didn't really change.

I just kept living as I had been until about six months later, when my hand suddenly started hurting. I decided to try entrusting that to my foundation, but it kept bothering me, so I finally went to see a doctor. Nothing they tried seemed to help, and I was finally diagnosed with bone marrow cancer. The doctor used several treatments, but my body didn't respond to any of them. Finally, he wanted to retest me for everything.

At that moment, I wanted nothing more than to completely rely upon my foundation. No more would I go to the hospital looking for hope. I just stayed home, enduring the pain. About two weeks went by like this, when I saw that you were having a large, public Dharma talk in Busan.

I went to the Busan Hanmaum Seon Center to see you, and as I waited, the thought arose, "Ah! Now my hand is going to be completely fine!" As soon as I had that thought, I was able to completely let go of all my fears and worries. And the moment I did see you, it felt like electricity was flowing through my body. A few days later, a boil appeared on my hand, and I ended up squeezing a lot of pus from it. It healed completely after a few days, and the pain has since vanished. My doctor wanted me to have more tests and treatments, but I know my hand is fine. Thank you so much.

Kun Sunim   Regardless of who you are, regardless of your position in society, education, gender, or age, every one of you has this incredible fundamental mind within you. If you just have faith in it, and rely upon it, you can move mountains, penetrate the secrets of the universe, and stop army tanks in their tracks.

But if you don't have faith in it, if you try to ignore it, then life is like trying to walk through an endless field of mud. Or flailing through the air, unable to get your feet under you. Please work on firmly trusting this inherent foundation of yours, so that you will be able to step beyond the boundaries of this middle world and become forever free.

Know that this inherent mind can take care of whatever you are going through! Believe in your inherent essence! [Thrusting her fist in the air.] This is where you can find courage! And vision and determination! Here is the power to turn the world upside down or to set it right!

Right now we are lame in one leg, blind in one eye, and deaf in one ear. Even the most advanced technology in the world, like lasers and such, can't compare to this ability of your inherent essence. Why? Because those are limited to the material world, to only one side of things. But this light within you is connected to both sides, as well as all the energy of the universe.

So leave behind thoughts of social status or judgements about others, and work together as brothers and sisters in the Dharma. The Buddha awakened to the reality that everyone else was also himself, so even cleaning someone else's bottom after a bowel movement was no more than cleaning his own. Should even a dog, sick with disease, raise from its foundation a deep desire for help, Buddha transforms into a dog and helps cure the disease, or frees the dog from its ignorance.[24] Here, "Buddha"

---

24. In this case, ignorance means the unenlightened habits that caused that dog to be born as a dog, thus, "freeing it from its ignorance" can mean helping the dog so it can move forward and grow, or it can even mean helping it to peacefully leave its body and then helping it to be reborn in better circumstances or at a higher level of existence.

does not refer to an individual, but rather to the great pillar of energy that is the whole.

Every single one of us has this incredible, formless mind, this one great pillar that encompasses everything, which the ancients called the "Highest Heaven of Mt. Sumeru." Take this pillar as your center, and strengthen your ability to let go. Develop your ability to entrust it with everything. In this way, let's take all suffering, all illness, every kind of karmic state of consciousness, and burn it all up!

Dharma Talk 2

The Healing Power of Our Inner Light

October 16, 1994

This talk was first published in English
as Volume 14 in the ongoing series,
Practice in Daily Life.

Everyone! You, me, the sunims here, and all Buddhas are inherently connected as one through this foundation we all have. To see you here, on this rainy day,[25] making such efforts to learn more about this and experience it for yourselves, well, it warms my heart.

If it were raining so heavily that people might be hurt, then we should all deeply input the thought that the rain should stop. Yet, today isn't so bad, and, from one perspective, coming here in the rain has been a good opportunity for you to exercise your determination! You are all so wonderful! In a way, I think you are more devout than sunims. Thank you.

As I'm always telling you, there is something very fundamental that encompasses the whole universe, including time as well. And this fundamental essence is directly connected to our center, our foundation, and functions as one with

---

25. This was a very large, outdoor Dharma talk.

it. The only difference between this fundamental essence of the universe, and your fundamental essence, is the scale of their functioning. They don't exist apart.

If you live in accord with this, then the path you need will exist right there in the middle of all the stuff you're experiencing each moment.

All lives and things have this foundation to them. And through this foundation, we are connected to each other, and so can communicate and work together with everything in both the visible realms as well as the unseen realms.

You may wonder why I'm talking about things you already know, but it's because this foundation, and the fact that we have it, is what makes everything else in our world possible. It's what connects everything and holds it together.

As it says in the *Flower Garland Sutra*, each and every living thing, along with each and every place, has this centered, fundamental mind of its own. This is often given different names, and so people mistake it for some kind of outside entity.

It's the unique centered mind of each living being, and each area, that is responsible for managing and taking care of that. The fundamental essence of each is connected to every other, exchanging energy and always communicating. And, according to the needs of the times, if these all become one and work together, they can become a truly great energy.

Further, if you make this fundamental mind your center, then outside things dare not enter, and those harmful things latent within you will just sleep quietly, not daring to manifest.

If you don't gather everything together into this one place and raise it up, what happens? You can't gather energy together. It's like there is nobody home, like the owner of the house has stepped out and left everything unlocked. So, others can freely wander in and out, tearing the place apart. Spirits of the dead wander in and try to live there, and all kinds of other problems related to germs, karmic states of consciousness, and the conditioned nature of existence start manifesting every which way. All of which ends up tearing apart your body and spirit.

Although everyone is endowed with this fundamental mind, if you don't raise it up, it can't perform its role. You have to give rise to the thought to do this, in order for that to happen.

Even though you managed to be born into this world, if you don't raise the intention to address whatever is confronting you, then nothing will happen. It's only after you give rise to a thought that you can take some action.

Even if there were unlimited electricity available, you couldn't draw upon that and use it without first giving rise to the intention to use it. Like the relationship between a house, a light bulb, and the power grid, all beings and things are connected through this foundation that we all have. But, if you don't give rise to the intention, you can't turn on the light – you can't put it to work. Only after giving rise to the intention to use that energy, can you draw upon it and use it as needed. The workings of this foundation are the basis of everything in the material world, as well as all sciences and philosophies.

The workings of your foundation underlie everything in your daily life. This is why we always say that you have to practice with what's right here in your daily life. What could you hope to find by ignoring this and looking around somewhere else?

But even your daily life is happening because you were born into this world. You're experiencing all kinds of good and bad things because you are here. It's you! Because you exist, you can experience all those things. It's you who encounters others, who meets the Buddha, and who experiences the world. None of this would matter if we hadn't been born, but since we're already here, shouldn't we try to leap as far and as high as we can?

This is why I'm always telling you that you have to start with yourself, and gather everything together into this fundamental mind of yours. Although everyone has this, instead of raising it up and putting it forward, they often just spend their time leading dissolute lives.

Above, this centered mind reaches all the universe, and below, it is firmly connected to all the earth. To put it another way, it's like a pillar reaching through all realms, connected to absolutely everything. But nonetheless, if you haven't raised it up, you can't draw upon its energy.

It penetrates all realms, and, like the axle of an old-fashioned cart, it provides the strength that allows us to function without hindrance. Raising up this fundamental mind is what guides us and allows us to work together with the energy of the universe.

I'm telling you this because we, as well as everything else, are one connected whole that is continuously reacting to each other. Big, small, wide, narrow, doing well, doing badly – all of this changes according to what we do and the thoughts we give rise to. When we bring forward this fundamental mind of ours, it connects with the foundation that penetrates the heavens and the earth, and that energy becomes available to be used as needed. And as we respond with this energy to the needs of the world, we naturally fulfill the roles of the Bodhisattvas.

In becoming this great mind, where the past, present, and future all function together as one, there's no place for anything to stick to. Karma, genetics, microbes, ghosts, whatever – all of these will fall asleep. Yet people who don't bring forward their fundamental mind will likely have a different experience of life.

I'm sorry if I repeat myself, but although we're all inherently endowed with this fundamental mind, you have to practice and give rise to the thought that you want this essence to come forward. All your thoughts and feelings are ready to work together as one, and when you rely upon this essence and entrust it with all of those things, it makes that happen. With everything working together as one, how could dust or grime not be transformed? When people practice relying upon their fundamental mind, how could delusions or problems caused by genetics, karma, or the conditioned nature of existence exist as some separate thing that could cause suffering?

Do you have any idea how great your mind is? A single thought of yours can cross the entire universe in an instant. The speed of light is nothing by comparison. Even light can only move so fast and no faster. And, it can only go where there's nothing; it is easily blocked. But your mind is infinitely faster; one thought from your foundation can enter the ground or the water and look all around.

How can words possibly describe all of this? Yet I have to use words anyway, to try to get people pointed in the right direction. So even if what I say sounds strange, please try to listen with an open mind and wisdom. Even though I only talk about one thing, know that there are ten more points connected to that. As I said before, if we don't practice relying upon our fundamental mind, and don't try to bring this fundamental mind forward, we end up as empty houses.

Everything about how you're living is automatically input into your foundation and recorded there. Later it all ruthlessly comes back out. Whatever you're experiencing, whether it's related to karma or to ghosts, all of that is automatically coming out according to how it was input. There's nowhere you can hide from this. Although it's true that the past doesn't exist because it's already gone, and the future doesn't exist because it hasn't come yet, right now, all of these karmic echoes are within you and keep relentlessly coming out again and again. So where could you hide? Even if you crawl inside of a barrel and pull the lid in tight after you, they'll still find you.

However, if we can bring forward this fundamental mind, so that it can work together with the foundation of the entire universe, then even if those kinds of things arise, they won't cause any problems. Should some problem occur nonetheless, you'll be able to take care of it immediately.

But if there is no owner in your home, then any passing spirits can enter and live there as if it were their own home. Sometimes people encounter spirits because of past karma, and sometimes it happens through a chance encounter with a spirit who is stuck where they died.

Spirits may cling to the place they died, especially in the case of car accidents, or, if they died in the mountains, they may have been trying to live in a tree. When these kinds of spirits meet a person who is an empty house, they try to move in, thinking that space is available.

Even though you probably can't see things like this, they're happening all the time. So on top of all the other things that are caused by past input, if you're living like an empty house, you may have other problems caused by spirits trying to wander in. Doctors and hospitals can easily treat illnesses that have ordinary causes, but they are helpless in the face of problems caused by karma and spirits.

Worse, if one spirit can enter you, then others can as well. So some people end up with two or three spirits living in their body, as if it were the spirits' own home. So, from the outside, it seems like the person will say one thing, but then follow that with something completely unrelated. They may shout out weird things like, "This is mine!" or "Get out!" They'll seem crazy, and their body often becomes ruined.

Those spirits will all be trying to tell them to do different, contradictory things, like, "Go here!" "Do this!" "Stop!" Struggling to deal with this becomes exhausting and harder to resist. So not only does the person suffer, but the people in their lives also have a hard time. This is what can happen if we lose our sense of centeredness.

As we've lived and evolved, we've had all kinds of shapes and created all sorts of karmic effects. Sometimes we experience these as they arise within us, and sometimes those effects come to us from the outside. But since those karmic echoes aren't things we can easily see and differentiate, we often mistake them for our own thoughts and feelings. We assume those are "me." Or, if someone hears a voice say, "I'm your dead cousin," they tend to believe it because they're unable to see what's really at work.

If you have a problem that's arisen from the unseen realm, then that very same unseen realm is where you have to solve it. If you've raised unwise thoughts toward others, and are now suffering because of those, then the solution, too, lies in how you use your mind. If you are suffering because of ghosts, then the solution lies in helping the ghosts move forward. But you won't have a clue about how to do all of this if you aren't relying upon your foundation.

Without this, there is no lasting way to take care of any of these problems. It all comes down to how you use your mind. Success, growth, and warmth all begin with you. As do failure, decline, and suffering.

This is why Sakyamuni said to know yourself first. If you know yourself, if you have faith in your inherent foundation and awaken to it, then you will be able to understand the workings of the entire universe. Then you can become free. If you can live as a true, free person, you are a Buddha, and a single thought of yours will manifest into the world and become reality. You will be able to freely respond to the needs of everyone and everything you encounter.

So, how could you turn your back on this practice? I hope that none of you will step back from this practice because of foolish thoughts such as, "How could someone like me ever understand what the Buddha said?"

You have to awaken to the deep implications and ability that the Buddha talked about, and then pay attention to the world and respond in a way suitable to these changing times. In some ways, it would be nice if we could just practice with a *hwadu*[26] like in the old days. But in this era, when you can view the entire world from your living room, if you practice like that, you'll just pass your days without anything to show for it.

---

26. Hwadu(話頭) (C. –hua-tou, J. –koan)**:** Traditionally, the key phrase of an episode from the life of an ancient master, which was used for awakening practitioners, and which could not be understood intellectually. This developed into a formal training system using several hundred of the traditional 1,700 koans.

However, hwadus are also fundamental questions arising from inside that we have to resolve. It has been said that our life itself is the very first hwadu that we must solve.

Actually, being born into this world is itself a hwadu. "What led you to being reborn here?" "What are you truly doing now?" And, "Where are you headed?" These are the questions you have to start with. You can discover the answers to them only when you are relying upon your foundation. So, if you're not entrusting everything to your foundation, and are only begging for things or pursuing your own well-being, then no matter how much you do this, Buddha won't respond to you. Not even the tiniest bit. Because you aren't communicating with Buddha.

The pathway, the channel, lies through your fundamental mind. So, focus on your fundamental mind and return everything there, and from this place, respond to whatever arises in your life. What if you could take care of all your difficulties freely and easily? This is how you can do it.

Relying on your fundamental mind isn't praying to the Buddha or begging him for something. Because everything arises from your root, return everything you experience back there. Take what it is that you seem to need, and entrust that as well. "Ah. Okay, true self, it's you that's doing everything, so you're the one that can take care of this." "Juingong, let me and others all work together harmoniously." "It's you that leads me towards awakening and shows me how to manifest wisdom.

If you entrust everything to this root of ours, then, because it's connected to everything else, it can evaluate that and will know what's good for you and what isn't, and won't let you go down a harmful path. If you're continuously entrusting everything to this place, then an intention entrusted there will also manifest into the world.

In other words, when the heavens, the earth, and yourself are functioning as one, this whole will take your intention and respond in a harmonious way. A single thought like this can manifest into the world and move the whole! This is the *Dharma*,[27] which you can taste and experience for yourself!

---

27. Dharma: This refers to both ultimate truth, and the truth taught by the Buddha.

Practicing like this, you can take care of every sort of thing you might encounter. Evil actions by others, corruption, disease, whatever. But this is only possible by relying upon your own root.

I'm not sure how well you'll be able to understand this, but I'd like to talk about one more thing before we take questions today.

So to speak, this thing that penetrates the heavens and the earth, and which is connected to humans' centered mind, is perhaps best described as a form of energy. It's like a pillar of fire or a support pillar that's beyond anything you can imagine. Even though it doesn't seem to move, it sends out infinite ability.

For example, if you're ill, and you give rise to the thought that, "It's my foundation, and only my foundation, that can truly take care of this disease," and entrust this thought to your foundation, then it's as if the hand of the Medicine Bodhisattva reaches out from this pillar of fire. When that connects to the one who is sick, the problems of that disease disappear.

Because it can send out unlimited energy, in any form imaginable, it's like it is full of uncountable Buddhas and Bodhisattvas. If you feel like someone's life is coming to an end too soon, and you entrust the thought that it should be longer, then it's as if the Buddha of the *Northern Dipper*[28] comes out and connects with them, and, circumstances permitting, may even make it possible in some cases to lengthen the span of their life. If you take the situations and emotions that confront you, and, as they arise, entrust them to this pillar of fire, then, the functions and energy we associate with names such as *Ksitigarbha*,[29] the mountain god, the god of the

---

28. Northern Dipper: (Also known as the Big Dipper.) Traditionally in Korea, people have believed that the seven stars of the Northern Dipper govern the length of humans' lives.

29. Ksitigarbha Bodhisattva (地藏菩薩)**:** The guardian of the earth who is devoted to saving all beings from suffering, and especially those beings lost in the hell realms.
Bodhisattva: In the most basic sense, Bodhisattva is the applied energy of our fundamental nature, used to help save beings. It can also be described as the non-dual wisdom of enlightenment being used to help beings awaken for themselves.
It is also depicted as a person of great spiritual ability who is dedicated to saving those lost in ignorance and suffering.

ocean, the god of the forest, and so on, will come forth and connect with you as needed.

To look at it another way, consider the atom. Even within a single atom, there are uncountable other particles. When some of those are separated out, they're given all sorts of different names, aren't they? Likewise, the "particles" that come from this pillar of fire are given names such as "Ksitigarbha," "Buddha of the *Seven Stars*,"[30] and so on. They respond instantly with the form that you need, and guide you forward. This sounds far-fetched, doesn't it?

When we are completely grounded in our fundamental mind, and it is deeply connected to this pillar of fire, this state can also be called Buddha. A thought raised from this state of Buddha can manifest and assume any kind of form or function. It can become *Aksobhaya*, *Amitabha*,

---

30. The Seven Stars is another name for the Northern Dipper.

Ksitigarbha, or *Avalokitesvara*.[31] That thought will automatically respond to people's needs, manifesting with a suitable form.

For example, if you're drowning, and from this deep place within, you think of the god of waters, then that thought manifests and functions as the god of waters.

However, if your thought doesn't connect with this deep place, then it won't manifest, and nothing will respond to it. This is true for even a Buddha. If he or she has a thought, but doesn't entrust it to this deep place, then that thought can't become Dharma, it can't manifest into the world.

This is why I'm always telling you that the source is within you. If you raise a thought through this foundation, then that thought becomes reality.

---

31. Aksobhaya(阿閦如來)**:** The Buddha of the Eastern Paradise, and counterpart of Amitabha Buddha.
Amitabha(阿彌陀)**:** The Buddha of the Western Pure Land, who teaches those reborn there and helps them attain Buddhahood.
Avalokitesvara Bodhisattva(觀世音菩薩)**:** The Bodhisattva of Compassion, who hears and responds to the cries of the world and delivers unenlightened beings from suffering.

It begins to manifest and function within your own day to day life. The teachings of the Buddha aren't some separate thing; rather, they are descriptions of the functioning of your ordinary, daily life. Right there in your boring life, with your family, work, and society, is where you can find Buddha, the path, and the inspiration to awaken. All the parts of your life are exactly the materials you need for your practice.

There are lots of people who study the sutras in order to learn the teachings of Buddha, but you need to first be diligently working at relying upon your fundamental mind. Then when you look at the sutras, you'll be able to realize their vast and incredible essence. The sutras were intended to help us learn and grow in our daily life. But in order to get any benefit from them, reading must go hand in hand with the careful observation and entrusting of your own thoughts and emotions; then you can connect with the sutras' deep meanings and understand how to forward in your daily life.

But if you just try to read the sutras without practicing like this, you won't be able to see their deeper teachings or to free your mind. Thus, you'll be at the mercy of your thoughts and emotions, and will often be overwhelmed by the things that confront you.

Even though people have been born at the human level, they still have so many different levels of spiritual development. To compare them to dishes, some people are like small bowls for soy sauce, others are plates or soup bowls, and still others are salad bowls. If someone is at the level of a soy sauce bowl, then that's all they can ever hold, isn't it? If you're at the level of a plate, all you can hold is cooked vegetables and such.

So practice hard and become a bowl so big that it can hold oceans! Take everything you feel and confront, and entrust it to this pillar of fire. For whatever goes in there is melted down and becomes one. No matter what kind of water flows into the ocean, it becomes ocean. If you take out a bucketful of water, no hole is left behind, and if you add a bucketful of water, it is instantly absorbed.

Moreover, the way of the ocean is to circulate and purify whatever enters it, all the while feeding and supporting beings beyond measure. Our mind, too, can become a great ocean.

This mind of ours! For example, you all have the ability to leave your body here and go visit your home and look around. All this is done in an instant, faster than even the speed of light. But if you diligently practice relying upon this foundation of ours, then what you'll see will not be just the surface appearances. Now you'll also be able to see all of the deep aspects of what's happening there. This practice is so precious!

Of course, these kinds of things should only be done when there is a strong need for them. Why? Because although impressive, these kinds of abilities aren't actually the path.

As Sakyamuni Buddha said, seeing the whole world in an instant is not the way to enlightenment and freedom, hearing people a hundred miles away isn't this path, visiting other places without moving your body isn't the path, nor is being able to know the thoughts of creatures from insects to human beings. Knowing the past lives of everyone you meet isn't the path, nor is obtaining all the five subtle powers.

Do you know why? Even if you can hear or see more than others, or go anywhere without moving your body, so what? None of those move you any closer to ultimate freedom. Being able to give water to a thirsty person is the path, as is being able to drink water yourself when you are in need. [Pointing to the cup beside her.] Even if I know there's water in this cup, if I can't pick that up, if I can't drink it, then what use is that knowledge?

Only when you can help others to drink, and also drink yourself, well, only that is the path. You have to be free from attachment to all those kinds of abilities that I mentioned. Only then can you freely use them as needed. This ability itself is called

Nujin,[32] but even that name is already gone. On this path, there is no fixed thing you can call "the Path."

Even though you could have just stayed home today, you made the effort to come here on this rainy day so that you could learn and practice. I want you to know just how beautiful I think this is. Long ago, when I was practicing on my own in the forests, I'd been sitting in a valley when the monsoon rains came. It was like the heavens exploded and almost immediately the stream near where I was sitting overflowed and covered the area with water. As the flowing water pushed against me, and the rain fell so hard that the brim of my straw hat collapsed around my head, I started laughing.

Although this rain could ruin my hat, although it could drown me, it couldn't get into my bones,

---

32. Nujin (漏盡通)**:** This is the state where one is free of all the things that cause suffering, where one is never caught by any thing or situation. It is also described as the state where one is not caught or entangled by even the five subtle powers, and so one is able to use them freely, as needed.

it couldn't get into my flesh, and it couldn't get into my mind. I suddenly felt so happy! That rain became an opportunity for a great experience in my practice.

Isn't everything a chance to practice and grow? So don't get caught up in narrow views like, "It shouldn't rain where so many have come to learn the teachings of Buddha!" So what if there's rain? You have to know what it tastes like when it rains, and the taste of when it doesn't rain.

You have to know both sides, both when and how things go well, and when and how they go badly. Only then can you take care of everything. If you go to Busan, you also have to know how to return. If you drive a car somewhere, you also have to be able to step out and walk away from it. Driving for a while, getting out, doing something, and then getting back in is the normal way of it, isn't it? If someone only knows how to get in and drive, but not how to get out again, well, that would be a strange kind of life.

So if it rains, take that as your practice. If it doesn't rain, take that, too, as your practice. Learn to take everything as a target to focus your practice on.

If I talk for too long today, you may lose sight of the point I want to make, so think of one thing that I've said today that really connected with you, and make an effort to memorize that. Then, go forward and try to apply that to your life.

When it seems hard to do, or you aren't really feeling it, go through the motions anyway! Keep working at it, and the imitation will become the real thing. And someday you will become a true Buddha. Keep this in mind, and diligently apply the point from this talk that seems to connect with you.

Now, are there any questions?

Questioner 1 (female)   Hello. For the last ten years I've had all kinds of different aches and pains, but the doctors all say I'm fine. I've really suffered from this, and now, on top of it all, my vision has become so bad that I can barely see in front of me. The doctors said that my optic nerve has withered, but there's nothing they can do about it. Please, help me with this if you can.

Kun Sunim   Entrust it all to your foundation, that's the one who is in charge of everything. You need to realize that your true self can show you the way. Have faith in it, and entrust it with all things. Like the person behind the wheel of a car, it's your mind that moves and steers your body. So if you have this thought, you go this way. With that thought, you go that way.

For example, when the doctors give a diagnosis, people tend to cling to that. When they do this, it becomes input, and so they have a harder time moving away from those words. This is why it's critical that you know how to break up those attachments. If you have faith that your foundation is doing everything, and if you're taking what you are experiencing and entrusting it back there, then your condition will begin to improve.

Have faith that everything arises from your foundation, and that it is also the very essence that can guide and take care of you. If you entrust everything to your foundation like this, your issues will be resolved before too long.

Questioner 2 (female)　My husband is fortunate in that he has a job, but it's very hard for him because he has asthma, and has trouble walking far. I would like to ask if you can cure him.

Kun Sunim　I'm not the one who cures those things. Even when it's someone else who's sick, entrust that illness to your essence. Then, because your essence, your foundation, and his are connected, if you are entrusting everything on this side, the light bulb on that side will turn on. Believe it. And teach your husband about entrusting and observing.

This is how you can take care of your own health, as well as your husband's. Further, as you practice like this, your children will become more grounded, and your family more harmonious. They'll be like plants whose roots have gotten stronger.

Questioner 3 (female)   Hello. When people have asked you about how to respond to various illnesses or difficult situation, you've told them to have faith in their foundation, and to entrust everything there and observe. How can entrusting like this cure things like diseases?

Kun Sunim   Your foundation, Juingong, is like the CEO who manages a company. If the CEO gives a command, the consciousnesses of all the lives within your body respond to that. Those consciousnesses respond and work together, or not, according to the decisions you give rise to.

If you don't give your employees a clear idea of what needs to be done, because you lack confidence and never make a firm decision, how could they ever accomplish anything? Just like this, if you make up your mind to fully entrust everything to your foundation, then all of the beings within your body will follow the instructions from your foundation, and that illness can be cured.

Questioner 4 (female)   My child has heart disease, but none of the doctors can agree about how severe it is, or what needs to be done. They're all telling us to do different things. I have to make a decision soon, but I have no idea which course would be best. I would like to ask for your teachings on this matter.

Kun Sunim   Although a doctor's help may yet be necessary, if you learn about entrusting everything to your foundation, and diligently work at this, then your child's condition will improve. In your case, it's possible that your child's condition isn't particularly urgent yet. There's also a good chance his disease can be healed if you practice entrusting.

It's quite a difficult thing when doctors have to operate on a child's brain or heart. If that becomes necessary, fully entrust the situation to your foundation. Then, even though the doctor operates, it's as if that's being done by the hands of your Juingong. If you can do this, the result will probably be pretty good.

Questioner 5 (female)   About five years ago, I started to hurt everywhere, and to feel very unsettled and anxious. I went to the hospital and was diagnosed with allergies. Although I've been treated for those, nothing really seems to get better. I'm still in pain and feel fearful. What should I do?

Kun Sunim   You have to rely upon your foundation. Whenever you realize that you're caught up in your pain or suffering, remember what I'm going to say and entrust this to your foundation: "True self, because even this illness ultimately arose from you, you can take care of it. You have to guide me and keep this body healthy."

In addition to working at this, you also need to work very hard at helping others, selflessly and with your whole heart. In your case, to put it simply, your body is filled with debt collectors looking to get paid. They're sitting there waiting for you to make good on your debts. Much of what you've received in the past was due to the *virtue and merit*[33] of your parents and ancestors. You needed to repay that, but haven't, so this problem has become very deep-rooted. To dissolve it, you have to pay your debts.

---

33. Virtue and merit(公德)**:** Here this term refers to the results of helping people or beings unconditionally and non-dually, without any thought of self or other. It becomes virtue and merit when you "do without doing," that is, doing something without the thought that "I did such and such." Because it is done unconditionally, all beings benefit from it.

Questioner 5   Okay. I'm reading about relying upon my foundation, but somehow I'm having a hard time remembering to do it.

Kun Sunim   That's because the debt collectors within you are still unsatisfied. There is a specific part of your debt that can only be repaid through giving and helping, and you haven't done that yet. Be grateful, help others with what they need, and let go of "I," while relying upon your foundation.

Questioner 5   Thank you.

Questioner 6 (male)   When I'm sick or hurting, I first turn to medicine, and then at the next stage, go to the doctor. But you've said today that we should first rely upon our foundation. Can you please say some more about this for people like me whose habit is to immediately turn to medicines or doctors?

Kun Sunim   Your question reminds me of when I lived in a hermitage below Sangwon Temple (in the Chiak Mountains). People used to come by the hundreds, asking for my help, mostly with illnesses. Because it was hard to get any kind of medicine in those days (around 1960),[34] there were so many who were in pain.

At that time, I stayed inside, with the door shut and people standing outside would just say what was wrong or what they needed, and then leave.[35] Then or now, and regardless of the illness, there's no hard and fast rule about taking medicine being right or wrong.

---

34. This was less then ten years after the country had been devastated by the Korean War. Very little infrastructure had been rebuilt, and country was still extremely poor. In 1960, the per capita income was less than US$80, versus $3,000 for the US.

35. This hermitage was a tiny hut. It was just one small room, about 140cm by 100cm, with a door made from wood lattice covered with thick paper. Many people left offerings, but Kun Sunim gave all of that to Sangwon Temple, and it was this money that paid for the 1960 reconstruction of the temple. At 1,200m above sea level, Sangwon Temple is the second highest temple in Korea, so construction was not easy or inexpensive.

There are two aspects you should understand about this issue. The first is, when you have such complete faith in your essence, Juingong, then it already knows what's going on, and the question of entrusting or not entrusting doesn't even arise. So when something about your health or body is a problem, Juingong naturally responds with the appropriate solution.

Your body is a device that your foundation has made, so it naturally knows what's needed to make urgent repairs. Think of something that comes from a factory – the workers who built it will also have the best idea about what can be done.

The second aspect is that when you have complete faith and also understand the workings of your foundation, then whether you go see a doctor or take medicine, to you it's no different from having a meal. If the thought of some medicine or treatment naturally arises, and it feels like that would be just right, then everything else in your body will be feeling the same way, and easily accept that.

If you look at it and the feeling arises that you really don't want to eat it, then even if you did, it would be of no benefit to you. For those people who are deeply relying upon their foundation, thoughts like these are not just random thoughts; they are the workings of their foundation. To get to this point, you have to entrust things so sincerely that there is no trace left of "I have done something." If you take medicine, entrust that so deeply that no trace of "taking" remains.

Even if you kill a cow for food, completely entrust any dualistic thoughts about killing, then you can also melt away the cow's ignorance, and guide it to be reborn at a higher level. You can do this on the spot.

So if you are only relying on medicine, you aren't working on connecting with your foundation, and can only cling to other people while hoping for the best.

Think about this: you came into being because of your fundamental essence, and this is what's enabling you to live right now, so doesn't it make sense that you should have faith in it? It takes only the smallest things to turn your flesh into a corpse. What keeps your body healthy is your fundamental mind, so if you're trying to rely upon something else, what good could result?

Even though you take medicine with the thought that, "Only my foundation can take care of this," if you don't actually have deep faith in your foundation, that intention can't be communicated. And so that medicine's effectiveness will likely be limited.

I'm not saying to not take medicine, just that our fundamental mind is the most important aspect, and that you have to fully rely upon it. Whether something functions as medicine or not depends upon how you use your mind. Isn't food also a medicine? Because people eat all the time, they don't think of food as a medicine. Yet food sustains our body. Food is medicine, water is medicine, everything is medicine. What isn't a medicine? If you eat something that makes you feel more healthy, isn't that a medicine?

Yet there is a stupid debate in your head that says if you use medicine, then that means your faith is weak. And so, you won't get better. And you keep going back and forth between thoughts like these.

Everything in this world starts from your foundation. People who complain that even though they look and look for Juingong, they can't find it, are missing the point. It is your own foundation, Juingong, that brought you into existence. Because the cow exists, the cart moves. If there was no cow, how could the cart have ever moved?

Questioner 6 Okay. Thank you for your teaching.

Questioner 7 (female) Hello, this is the third Dharma talk of yours I've attended. My brother is fifty-two years old, and has been sick for the last seven years. My seventy-nine-year-old mother has been taking care of him all this time. As the years have stretched out, they've both become exhausted and often end up fighting with each other. So I'm here to ask you to cure my brother.

Kun Sunim   This isn't a hospital. What did the doctors say?

Questioner 7   That he has liver problems.

Kun Sunim   Everyone, there's something you really have to know, if you don't already: a lot of illnesses, perhaps eighty percent or more, have an unseen aspect related to our minds. But when people don't know about their fundamental mind, their physical body becomes their sole focus, and when something goes wrong, they look for an outward, physical solution.

If you run off to the hospital every time you have some discomfort, and demand this test or that procedure, eventually your body is going to end up being ruined. I'm sure doctors would have rude things to say about me if they heard this, but it's true. But, that said, I'm not saying to never go see a doctor.

Years ago one of the laymen here had a bad infection in his leg, and almost had to have it amputated. But after he started entrusting this to his foundation, almost miraculously, the infection, which had started at his ankle and spread up to his knee, began to retreat back down his leg, and his leg was saved. This was possible because he was so deeply sincere, and mind can connect with mind. Through his fundamental mind, he communicated with the minds of all the lives in his body, which then all worked together to relieve the infection. The doctors were so amazed, and asked him if he was religious, because they thought a miracle had happened.

If you have absolute faith in your root, Juingong, and entrust it with everything, then all the separate consciousnesses of the cells that make up your body can communicate with each other and will work together according to the thoughts you give rise to. When you are returning absolutely everything to this fundamental one mind and it all becomes part of the same whole, then those consciousnesses would never do anything that hurts the whole. Fingers on the same hand don't hurt each other. You need this truth in your life.

Like fingers, all the consciousnesses in our body are separate from each other, but there is this deep one mind that connects them all. If we raise this *pillar of mind* [36] and all those consciousnesses start working as one, how could they hurt each other? Further, they become willing to help each other in order to live. As they all become connected together, they begin to heal the parts that were breaking down.

Regardless of the disease or its seriousness, if all the consciousnesses in your body, right down to the cells in your marrow, work together as one, then whatever is wrong can be set right.

Yet when people hear labels such as "cancer" or "leukemia," a part of them instantly believes there's no hope and thinks they are already dead.

---

36. Pillar of mind: Similar to *Jujangja*(拄杖子), which is literally a monk's staff, but often implied to mean a grasp or reliance upon our fundamental mind.

Because they think that they're as good as dead, the lives within them also think that and give up. But, because this is so, it's also how you can help heal that disease. The truth and functioning of one mind is precious beyond words.

This is true for things outside our bodies as well. There is no "can" or "can't" here. This one mind of ours is inherently connected with everything, and has the potential to communicate instantly with anything, anywhere. Because of all this, it can guide and save every single sentient being.

Truly, it can save all beings, but they have to meet it partway. They have to work to break through the layers of what they have made over distant eons. Think of a kind heart as a bowl. If people haven't made even a tiny bowl, they can't receive anything. Not only can't anything be put in their bowl, no communications with this great one mind are possible, either.

To give another example, if you are wiring a lamp, you have to first strip off the layers of plastic on the ends, don't you? If you don't do that, will the light come on? No.

But, when you diligently work at entrusting everything that is confronting you, all of that will be melted down. Those layers will be peeled away, and energy and communications can flow back and forth.

Questioner 8 (female)   Hello. I was diagnosed with a brain tumor three years ago, and although I still have regular hospital visits, it's clear to me that my attitude is critically important.

The last few years have been really hard, and I want to finish with this and quickly recover. Before and after my operation, I was reciting the *Thousand Hands Sutra*,[37] and this helped me get through it. I've been coming to Hanmaum Seon Center on a regular

---

37. The Thousand Hands Sutra(千手經)**:** Daehaeng Kun Sunim's translation of this was published in English as *A Thousand Hands of Compassion*(2008). It is a traditional chanting text in Korean Buddhism, but Daehaeng Sunim translated it into Hangul by meaning, and in reciting it, we teach and remind ourselves of the basics of spiritual practice.

basis for only a month, but would you please give me a teaching to help strengthen and steady my mind?

Kun Sunim   It doesn't matter whether you've been coming here for a month or a year. What we've done in the past returns to us. Sometimes it returns as genetics, and sometimes it returns as karma that gets processed through the brain and sent out to the body.

But none of that is separate from this foundation that has made us. So entrust everything back to our foundation, Juingong, and know that it's what can truly sort out your old input and take care of your situation. Then, your tumor may gradually become smaller. But at any rate, before too long, your problems will become better.

This last time I went to San Francisco, I met a man named Roy from San Jose, who was the publisher of a magazine. He had come because he wanted to make a donation of a thousand dollars to the Seon Center. As we talked, he said that his son was suffering from a tumor, and would undergo an operation in the next few days. But, before then, the doctors couldn't know what kind of tumor it was or how severe it was. I took a deep look inside, and told him the following. His son actually had two tumors, one large and one small. But through this practice of entrusting, they could be shrunken, and the operation would go smoothly, with his son being released from the hospital in three days. It would depend upon him.

Some days later, Roy called and said that everything went exactly as I'd said. There were two tumors, both of which were removed without problems, and his son was released three days after the surgery.

Most of the time, doctors can only help you with thirty to forty percent of the problem; you have to take care of the rest. That's your share. The foundation that moves and guides you is where this has to be taken care of. But how can you handle that sixty-odd percent if you aren't looking towards your foundation? Are you going to waste your time believing in some world above the clouds? Are you going to put all your hopes on the actions of other people? Or hope that statues will magically solve your problems?

Believe in your own true self, your foundation. That's what enables you to move. That's the real you. You who came here today. You who interacts with others, who makes your way in the world. Believe in this, your own foundation. You already have all the ability and everything you need right here within you.

A while back, there was someone here who had throat cancer, and was so weak she could barely move. But, learning about this practice, she started entrusting everything to her foundation and relying upon it. As she did this, her cells began to function better, and eventually her life became normal again. Her life is happy now, and she even has a child.

You need to gather your courage and go forward calmly and peacefully. If you're searching outwardly for Avalokitesvara to come help you, your own, inner bodhisattva of compassion can't take care of you.

Questioner 9 (female) I'm glad I can speak with you today. I've always thought my practice was going fine, but it seems like that was just because I never faced any particular challenges. I didn't turn a sharp eye on myself and really look at how I was practicing.

About a month ago, I suddenly had to have an operation for pancreatic cancer. I was scared and worried, but when I heard you say to take everything that comes up and practice with it, that really helped.

I received my first chemotherapy treatments, but the doctors say that I have to get those once a month for the next ten years. But that treatment is really horrible, and I don't see how I can withstand it year after year. So, I wanted to ask you about this.

Kun Sunim Whether you undergo chemotherapy or not, don't worry about it. You're not the one who's taking care of this.

Questioner 9 I know, but it's hard not to worry.

Kun Sunim   All of the lives within your body are bodhisattvas. But you don't know this, and instead think that it's you who is sick, that it's you who is in pain, that it's you who goes through that hardship. Stop thinking that you have to go through this by yourself; instead, let all of the bodhisattvas within you help share that burden. When you raise the thought that, "Juingong, it's you who can prevent this suffering," and entrust this to your foundation, it will communicate with all the parts of your body. Then, having no pain or worries, whether you receive chemotherapy or not, aren't you doing just fine?

Questioner 9   Thank you so much!

Kun Sunim   Everyone, you all have the ability to take care of absolutely everything, but you're unable to simply because you don't know that you have this ability! Because you are made of earth, water, fire, and air, you are fully endowed with light, energy, magnetism, and can communicate with all the earth, water, fire, and air that exists anywhere. So practice and be able to make use of these abilities!

Questioner 9   As they were preparing me for the operation, I clung desperately to Juingong, and the operation went smoothly, and I didn't have any problems afterwards.

Kun Sunim   That's good! But you have to keep going and be able to communicate with your foundation.

Questioner 9   Thank you.

Kun Sunim   Anyway, please take care of yourself and live a healthy life. Science, philosophy, medicine, astrophysics – none of these exist apart from your one mind. If you're diligent in your practice, you'll see the results. But there's no deceiving your foundation. If you lie to yourself, nothing will happen.

Questioner 10 (female) Thank you for this chance to see you. I really appreciate your teachings about one mind.

A good friend of mine, who's like my own sister, was recently diagnosed with cervical cancer. The doctors have been treating it with radiation, but as a result, she has problems with her bladder and had to have a catheter with a bag put in. I gave her a book about this practice of one mind, and I think she's doing well at it. I'm entrusting her situation as well, but I guess that still hasn't been enough to help her recover.

I feel sorry for her, and came here with the hope that if you knew about her situation and entrusted it, then she might recover quickly.

Kun Sunim Look, I'm not a doctor. I think you should have faith that if something within you is wrong, then that which can fix it is also within you. But I don't think you do.

When people try to use radiation therapy to treat diseases without relying upon their own foundation, and only chasing after the physical issues, then about seventy percent of the time, they develop kidney or bladder problems, and their blood platelets are destroyed, so that they end up with all kinds of other diseases.

So, should there be a disease in your body, it would be best if you can leave your body alone and instead heal that illness from the inside, through the practice of relying upon your foundation.

Everybody owes a death. As long as you are going to die anyway, why put yourself through all kinds of extra pain? I've seen so many cases like this. What pitiful endings. Wouldn't it be better to peacefully leave your body?

But when you have faith in your foundation, and can communicate with the lives in your body so that they all work together, then, circumstances permitting, that disease can clear up. I've seen that happen before with women who had cervical cancer.

"That's not a huge deal," I'd say. "It came from your body, so don't you think this same body should be able to take care of it?" This is why I'm always telling people about how to rely upon their foundation. After hearing this and working at it, as soon as their bleeding stopped, they'd run to the doctor to make sure they were fine. [Sighs.]

Whether you live or die, why such a fuss? When your body is broken down and worn out, wouldn't it be better to trade it in for a new one?

Questioner 11 (male) I'd like to ask you about mental illness and cancer, both of which tend to be very hard to cure. You've often told us that diseases can be caused by ghosts, genetics, and past karma. And in modern medicine, doctors suspect cancer is caused by genetic problems related to cell division. With schizophrenia, they believe the cause may lie with genetic defects related to neurotransmitters. Of course, the effects of things like ghosts and karma would be beyond their ability to detect.

If I've understood you correctly, humans have lived for eons, eating others and being eaten in turn. They've created layer after layer of causes and effects since the time they were microbes. Thus, it seems like there are endless possibilities for those past causes to manifest, yet so many seem to get cancer or mental illnesses. Is there a particular reason for this?

Kun Sunim   The reasons are as different and numerous as the snowflakes that fall from the sky. Every reason is different because we've all lived different lives, and what we experience are the results of that. If you would pass through all of those causes without being hurt by them, then you have to make them one with yourself. You do that by returning everything to just one place.

These days, there are unspeakable tragic things happening around the world, even in Korea, aren't there? They're so terrible, and yet so unbelievably absurd. For example, there were some children playing and something went terribly wrong, and one boy was killed with an iron fire poker. The dead child was reborn in the same village, and later ended up killing the friend who had accidentally killed him before. And he did it with an iron fire poker.

So, how could they have prevented this? How should it have been handled afterwards? The first step is to acknowledge that cause and effect plays a role. If we ignore this, then we miss one of the most effective ways to practice and awaken.

What is cause and effect? To give a simple example, if you speak gently, then you'll get back gentle words from others. If you yell and swear at others, then in turn you'll be hit by yelling and swearing.

To look at it from an even deeper level, there is no separate thing called "karma." Events just unfold, and for the sake of understanding and practice, the label "karma" was made. But it's not a real, separate thing.

Years ago, there was a farmer who came across a ball of baby snakes, and took a shovel and chopped them up. He would also roast and eat the larger snakes he came across. He did these things because he looked down on them, and thought their lives were worthless. In the old days, there were a lot more people who didn't understand this principle that we are all connected.

But even though someone doesn't know this, those actions are input within them and carried around with them. And will eventually come back out, affecting you, or your children. Those snakes, too, have a spirit, and if the farmer had been aware of this foundation that is the source of the snakes' spirit, he wouldn't have hurt them. And if the snakes had been aware of their own foundation, they wouldn't have sought revenge against the farmer. But the snakes were only aware of their pain, and who had hurt and abused them. So their spirit chased after the farmer, wanting to inflict pain and death on him and his family. It might be a year, or another lifetime, before the results of something like that catch up with a person.

This is why you have to know and be able to apply this truth of one mind, and resolve the things you are going through.

Questioner 11   Then, can I understand that those people with severe cancer or mental illness had created a lot more of these kinds of causes than other people?

Kun Sunim   Their existence itself is the result of how they've lived.

Questioner 11   I understand.

Kun Sunim So see everything nondually. Entrust it all unconditionally. Let go of all traces of "you" and "I," "good" and "bad," and be generous and giving with absolutely everyone!

Long ago, Sakyamuni Buddha had a disciple who was quite dim-witted. No matter how long the Buddha taught him, he still didn't seem to grasp anything. So, the Buddha gave him a broom and said, "Take this broom, and keep sweeping up everything. Don't miss a spot."

Please keep reflecting on this, and diligently practice returning to your own root.

Thank you.

Glossary

Aksobhaya (阿閦如來)

The Buddha of the Eastern Paradise, and counterpart of Amitabha Buddha.

Amitabha (阿彌陀)

The Buddha of the Western Pure Land, who teaches those reborn there and helps them attain Buddha-hood.

Avalokitesvara Bodhisattva (觀世音菩薩)

The Bodhisattva of Compassion, who hears and responds to the cries of the world and delivers unenlightened beings from suffering.

Bhikkunis

Female sunims who are fully ordained are called Bhikkuni(比丘尼) sunims, while male sunims who are fully ordained are called Bhikku(比丘) sunims. This can also be a polite way of indicating male or female sunims.

Bodhisattva

In the most basic sense, Bodhisattva is the applied energy of our fundamental nature, used to help save beings. It can also be described as the non-dual wisdom of enlightenment being used to help beings awaken for themselves.

It is also depicted as a person of great spiritual ability who is dedicated to saving those lost in ignorance and suffering.

Buddha

In this text, "Buddha" is capitalized out of respect, because it represents the fundamental enlightened essence we all have, along with its functioning. "The Buddha" always refers to Sakyamuni Buddha.

Buddha-dharma

This can refer to the fundamental reality that the teachings of Buddha point towards, or, occasionally, the teachings themselves.

Dharma

This refers to both ultimate truth, and the truth taught by the Buddha.

Dharma brother

A fellow practitioner. There is also a strong nuance of recognition of Vimalakirti as someone of impressive spiritual depth and standing.

Emptiness

Emptiness is not a void, but rather refers to the ceaseless flowing of all things. Everything is flowing as part of one whole, so there is nothing that can be separated out and set aside as if it existed independently of everything else. There is, therefore, no "me" that exists apart from other people or other things. There is only the interpenetrated and interdependent whole, "empty" of any independent or separate selves or objects.

Five subtle powers (五神通)

These are the power to know past and future lives, the power to know others' thoughts and emotions, the power to see anything, the power to hear anything, and the power to go anywhere.

Fundamental mind

This refers to our inherent essence, that which we fundamentally are. "Mind," in Mahayana Buddhism, almost never means the brain or intellect. Instead it refers to the essence through which we are connected to everything, everywhere. It is intangible, beyond space and time, and has no beginning or end. It is the source of everything, and everyone is endowed with it. "Fundamental mind" is interchangeable with other terms such as "Buddha-nature," "true nature," "true self," and "foundation."

Hanmaum [han-ma-um]

Han means one, great, and combined, while maum means mind, as well as heart, and together they mean everything combined and connected as one.

What is called Hanmaum is intangible, unseen, and transcends time and space. It has no beginning or end, and is sometimes called our fundamental mind. It also means the mind of all beings and everything in the universe connected and working together as one. In English, we usually translate this as one mind.

Hwadu(話頭) (C. –hua-tou, J. –koan)

Traditionally, the key phrase of an episode from the life of an ancient master, which was used for awakening practitioners, and which could not be understood intellectually. This developed into a formal training system using several hundred of the traditional 1,700 koans.

However, hwadus are also fundamental questions arising from inside that we have to resolve. It has been said that our life itself is the very first hwadu that we must solve.

Ignorance (無明)

In Buddhism, "ignorance" literally means darkness. It is the unenlightened mind that does not see the truth. It is being unaware of the inherent oneness of all things, and it is the fundamental cause of birth, aging, sickness, and death.

Juingong (主人空)

Pronounced "ju-in-gong." Juin(主人) means the true doer or the master, and gong(空) means empty. Thus Juingong is our true nature, our true essence, the master within that is always changing and manifesting, without a fixed form or shape.

Daehaeng Sunim has compared Juingong to the root of the tree. Our bodies and consciousness are like the branches and leaves, but it is the root that is the source of the tree, and it is the root that sustains the visible tree.

Karmic affinity (因緣)

The connection or attraction between people or things, due to previous karmic relation-ships.

Karmic consciousness

Our thoughts, feelings, and behaviors are recorded as the consciousnesses of the lives that make up our body. These are sometimes called karmic consciousnesses, although they don't have independent awareness or volition. Sometime afterwards, these con-sciousnesses will come back out.

Thus, we may feel happy, sad, angry, etc., without an obvious reason, or they may cause other problems to occur. The way to dissolve these consciousnesses is not to react to them when they arise, but instead to entrust them to our foundation. However, even these consciousnesses are just temporary combinations, so we shouldn't cling to the concept of them.

Ksitigarbha Bodhisattva (地藏菩薩)
The guardian of the earth who is devoted to saving all beings from suffering, and especially those beings lost in the hell realms.

Middle world
In Buddhism, the realm of human beings is sometimes described as the "middle realm" or the "middle world," because it said to be one of six realms. It exists below the realms of more advanced beings, called devas and asuras, but above the realms of animals, hungry ghosts, and the various hell states.

Mind(心)(Korean – maum)
In Mahayana Buddhism, "mind" refers to this fundamental mind, and almost never means the brain or intellect. It is intangible, beyond space and time, and has no beginning or end. It is the source of everything, and everyone is endowed with it.

Northern Dipper (Also known as the Big Dipper.)
Traditionally in Korea, people have believed that the seven stars of the Northern Dipper govern the length of humans' lives.

Nujin (漏盡通)

This is the state where one is free of all the things that cause suffering, where one is never caught by any thing or situation. It is also described as the state where one is not caught or entangled by even the five subtle powers, and so one is able to use them freely, as needed.

One mind (Hanmaum [han-ma-um])

From the Korean, where "one" has a nuance of great and combined, while "mind" is more than intellect and includes "heart" as well. Together, they mean everything combined and connected as one. What is called "one mind" is intangible, unseen, and transcends time and space. It has no beginning or end, and is sometimes called our fundamental mind. It also means the mind of all beings and everything in the universe connected and working together as one.

Pillar of mind

Similar to Jujangja(拄杖子), which is literally a monk's staff, but often implied to mean a grasp or reliance upon our fundamental mind.

Relying upon our fundamental mind

Trusting and relying upon our fundamental mind is the essence of spiritual practice and growth in all Daehaeng Kun Sunim's teachings. It's the foundation of all spiritual progress. We all have this Buddha-nature, this original face, this inherent mind, and, in fact, everything in our life revolves around it.

When teaching people about spiritual practice, Daehaeng Kun Sunim always emphasized that the very first step was just being aware that we all have this inherent nature. The next step was trying to rely upon it. This means taking what's confronting us, what's arising in our life, and doing our best to entrust that to this fundamental essence and then to let go of it. As we entrust something, we let go of it and just be aware, observing what's going on, without trying to watch too closely and see what happens.

As we keep working at this, we'll get experiences, times when everything seems to just click into place. We will experience times when we truly let go unconditionally, without a lot of "I" or "me," letting this inherent Buddha-nature take care of what we entrusted. As we see it working, as we experience this for ourselves, our faith in it naturally becomes deeper, and we are better able to entrust more and more. This practice of relying upon our fundamental mind, our Buddha-nature, is a self-correcting path that seems narrow in the beginning, but which eventually becomes a great highway.

Samsara

The endless cycle of birth and death that all living things are continuously passing through.

Seon(禪)(Chan, Zen)

Seon describes the unshakeable state where one has firm faith in their inherent foundation, their Buddha-nature, and so returns everything they encounter back to this fundamental mind. It also means letting go of "I," "me," and "mine" throughout one's daily life.

Sunim / Kun Sunim

Sunim is the respectful title of address for a Buddhist monk or nun in Korea, and Kun Sunim is the title given to outstanding nuns or monks.

The Thousand Hands Sutra (千手經)

Daehaeng Kun Sunim's translation of this was published in English as *A Thousand Hands of Compassion*(2008). It is a traditional chanting text in Korean Buddhism, but Daehaeng Sunim translated it into Hangul by meaning, and in reciting it, we teach and remind ourselves of the basics of spiritual practice.

True suchness

Here, Daehaeng Kun Sunim is saying that everything we encounter in our daily lives is the teachings of the truth (the Buddha-dharma), a method for awakening to the truth (such as meditation and kong-ans,) and the state of being one with the truth (true suchness.)

Universe

This includes all visible realms, as well as all unseen realms.

Vimalakirti

A lay disciple of Sakyamuni Buddha who was renowned for the depth of his enlightenment. His name means "Pure" or "Unstained." He appears in the Vimalakirti-Nirdesa Sutra, where he taught even the great disciples of the Buddha. He is portrayed as the ideal layperson, one who attained the essence of the Buddha-dharma and who thoroughly applied his understanding to his life. He would help those who were poor and suffering, and teach and educate those who were behaving badly.

Virtue and merit (公德)

Here this term refers to the results of helping people or beings unconditionally and non-dually, without any thought of self or other. It becomes virtue and merit when you "do without doing," that is, doing something without the thought that "I did such and such." Because it is done unconditionally, all beings benefit from it.

Other Books by Seon Master Daehaeng

English
- Wake Up And Laugh (Wisdom Publications)
- No River To Cross (Wisdom Publications)
- My Heart Is A Golden Buddha (Hanmaum Publications)
  Also available as an audiobook
- Standing Again (Hanmaum Publications)
- Sharing the Same Heart (Hanmaum Publications)
- Touching The Earth (Hanmaum Publications)
- A Thousand Hands of Compassion
  (Hanmaum Publications) [Korean/English]
- One Mind: Principles (Hanmaum Publications)
  All of these are available in paper or ebook formats

- Practice in Daily Life (Korean/English bilingual series)
  1. To Discover Your True Self, "I" Must Die
  2. Walking Without A Trace
  3. Let Go And Observe
  4. Mind, Treasure House Of Happiness
  5. The Furnace Within Yourself
  6. The Spark That Can Save The Universe
  7. The Infinite Power Of One Mind
  8. In The Heart of A Moment
  9. One With The Universe
  10. Protecting The Earth
  11. Inherent Connections
  12. Finding A Way Forward
  13. Faith In Action
  14. The Healing Power of Our Inner Light
  15. The Doctor Is In (New)
  16. Living the Good Life (Forthcoming)

Korean
- 건널 강이 어디 있으랴 (Hanmaum Publications)
- 내 마음은 금부처 (Hanmaum Publications)
- 처음 시작하는 마음공부1 (Hanmaum Publications)

Russian
• Дзэн И Просветление (Amrita-Rus)

German
• Wache Auf und Lache (Theseus)
• Umarmt von Mitgefühl (Deutsch·Koreanisch, Diederichs)
• Wie fließendes Wasser (Goldmann)
• Wie fließendes Wasser - CD (steinbach sprechende bücher)
• Vertraue und lass alles los (Goldmann)
• Grundlagen (Hanmaum Publications, New)

Czech
• Probuď se! (Eugenika)

Spanish
• Ningún Río Que Cruzar (Kailas Editorial)
• Una Semilla Inherente Alimenta El Universo (Hanmaum Publications)
• Si Te Lo Propones, No Hay Imposibles (Hanmaum Publications)
• El Camino Interior (Hanmaum Publications)
• Vida De La Maestra Seon Daehaeng (Hanmaum Publications)
• Enseñanzas De La Maestra Daehaeng (Hanmaum Publications)

Indonesian
• Sup Cacing Tanah (PT Gramedia)

Vietnamese
• Không có sông nào để vượt qua
  (Hanmaum Publications; Vien Chieu, Vietnam)
• tỉnh thức và cưới
  (Hanmaum Publications; Vien Chieu, Vietnam)
• Chạm mặt đất (Hanmaum Publications; Vien Chieu, Vietnam)

Chinese
• 我心是金佛（简体字）(Hanmaum Publications, 韩国)
• 无河可渡（简体字）(Hanmaum Publications, 韩国)
• 人生不是苦海（繁体字）(Hanmaum Publications, 韩国)
• 我心是金佛（繁体字）（橡树林文化出版，台湾）

Anyang Headquarters of Hanmaum Seonwon

1282 Gyeongsu-daero, Manan-gu, Anyang-si,
Gyeonggi-do, 13908, Republic of Korea
Tel: (82-31) 470-3175 / Fax: (82-31) 470-3209
www.hanmaum.org/eng
onemind@hanmaum.org

Overseas Branches of Hanmaum Seonwon

ARGENTINA
Buenos Aires
Miró 1575, CABA, C1406CVE, Rep. Argentina
Tel: (54-11) 4921-9286 / Fax: (54-11) 4921-9286
http://hanmaumbsas.org

Tucumán
Av. Aconquija 5250, El Corte, Yerba Buena,
Tucumán, T4107CHN, Rep. Argentina
Tel: (54-381) 425-1400
www.hanmaumtuc.org

BRASIL
São Paulo
R. Newton Prado 540, Bom Retiro
Sao Paulo, CEP 01127-000, Brasil
Tel: (55-11) 3337-5291
www.hanmaumbr.org

CANADA
Toronto
20 Mobile Dr., North York, Ontario M4A 1H9, Canada
Tel: (1-416) 750-7943
www.hanmaum.org/toronto

GERMANY
Kaarst
Broicherdorf Str. 102, 41564 Kaarst, Germany
Tel: (49-2131) 969551 / Fax: (49-2131) 969552
www.hanmaum-zen.de

THAILAND
Bangkok
86/1 Soi 4 Ekamai Sukhumvit 63
Bangkok, Thailand
Tel: (66-2) 391-0091
www.hanmaum.org/cafe/thaihanmaum

USA
Chicago
7852 N. Lincoln Ave., Skokie, IL 60077, USA
Tel: (1-847) 674-0811
www.hanmaum.org/chicago

Los Angeles
1905 S. Victoria Ave., L.A., CA 90016, USA
Tel: (1-323) 766-1316
www.hanmaum.org/la

New York
144-39, 32 Ave., Flushing, NY 11354, USA
Tel: (1-718) 460-2019 / Fax: (1-718) 939-3974
www.juingong.org

Washington D.C.
7807 Trammel Rd., Annandale, VA 22003, USA
Tel: (1-703) 560-5166
www.hanmaum.org/wa

If you would like more information about these books or
would like to order copies of them,
please call or write to:

Hanmaum International Culture Institute
Hanmaum Publications
1282 Gyeongsu-daero, Manan-gu, Anyang-si,
Gyeonggi-do, 13908,
Republic of Korea
Tel: (82-31) 470-3175
Fax: (82-31) 470-3209
e-mail: onemind@hanmaum.org
hanmaumbooks.org